# McKinley's Bulldog:
## The Battleship OREGON

# McKinley's Bulldog:
## The Battleship
## OREGON

### Sanford Sternlicht

Nelson-Hall
Chicago

Library of Congress Cataloging in Publication Data

Sternlicht, Sanford
    McKinley's bulldog, the battleship Oregon.

    Bibliography: p. 131
    Includes index.
    1.  Oregon (Battleship)   I.   Title.
VA65.07S74          359.3'2'520973          77–8603
ISBN 0–88229–263–3   (cloth)
ISBN 0-88229-516-0   (paper)

Manufactured in the United States of America.

# Contents

Preface    vii

1    The ABCD Navy    1

2    The Launching:
"Like Crested Pallus Armed"    15

3    At the Ready    29

4    The Captain and Castile    41

5    "Six Thousand Miles
to the Indian Isles"    55

6    Into Battle    71

7    Mopping Up    97

8    Disaster and Rescue    103

9    Fiasco and Final Glory    113

Appendix A    123

Appendix B    127

Notes    129

Bibliography    131

Index    133

# Preface

Port Merizo, Guam, languished under the mid-September sun. The heat waves rose like twisting, shimmering baroque columns from the quiescent sea, so that when viewed from seaward the scene—the huts on the beach, the jungle beyond, and the ancient volcanic hills that crowned the island and proclaimed its origin—took on the unreal quality of an old, faded postcard. It was 1944, and the Pacific war had twice flamed across the little island, destroying the town of Agana and many of the villages. The Japanese had sailed warships to Guam, a United States possession, and captured all the Americans by December 12, 1941. But, on July 20 of this year, the Americans had come back with many more ships, bombing and shelling with a vengeance as the terrified natives, the Chamorros—including the five hundred villagers of Merizo—hid in the hills. By August 9, the island was firmly in U.S. hands once more and the kindlier, less consistent, curious American rule again established. The villagers returned.

Guam no longer enjoyed the easy pace of life of happy, prewar days. The island throbbed with frantic energy, generated mostly by American seabees bulldozing long airstrips out of the jungle. Guam was needed as a base for the Superforts that would soon be hammering at the industrial cities of Japan herself. Already bombers were

making daily runs from Guam to attack more westerly
islands still in Japanese hands but destined to serve as
stepping stones on the road to victory.

Guam was secure, or at least the official communi-
qués had said so, and a piece of American territory—
taken from Spain by the United States cruiser *Charleston*
during the Spanish-American War—had been returned
to U.S. control. But some of the marines who had strug-
gled to wrest the island from the Japanese during the
bloody summer had been ordered to remain behind in the
wake of the war to carry out the mean, dirty anticlimax
called mopping up. They and the Chamorros of Merizo
both knew that Japanese survivors, well armed and organized into foraging patrols, still constituted a military
menace on the island. At any unguarded moment, a day-
dreaming marine or a seabee dozing off for a moment in
a shady clump of trees might find himself, for the remaining fraction of a second of his life, facing the business end of a Japanese bayonet held by a defeated but un-
conquered enemy soldier.

In the harbor one bright afternoon that September,
a strange hull, ironbound in what seemed to be a belt of
thick armor, was towed in under the escort of the LCI
gunship 474 and moored by a bow anchor and by chains
hauled out and bullnosed through a mooring buoy astern.
The officer-in-charge of the port and the commander of
Service Squadron 12 knew only that the vessel was the
IX 22, a nondescript old hulk pressed into service as a dynamite barge, loaded stateside with 1,400 tons of 60 percent gelatin plus a lot of other high explosives, and towed
out to Guam. The tow had been directed to Port Merizo
instead of the main harbor at Apra to keep the "super
firecracker" in quarantine—away from the other vessels
supplying the airfield and the base construction. LCT's
and LCVP's—the ubiquitous, workhorse "peter boats"—
were lying off awaiting signals to come alongside and
load dynamite for blasting at Apra and also for Tinian,
Saipan, and Palau.

When the sun had sunk in the western sea and the evening breeze had cooled the harbor somewhat, the boatswain's mate of the LCI led a working party on board the barge to post an armed guard on the bow and on the stern, rig searchlights for night off-loading, and set windscoops to get some air through the seven hatches and into the holds. The LCI sailors manned a deck winch and hauled a few boxes of the dynamite topside so that the gunner's mate could inspect the condition of the cargo after the long, hot voyage.

Just as the lids were removed, a burst of Japanese machine gun fire from the beach only seventy-five yards away sprayed the deck of the huge barge, and bullets danced among the terrified sailors flying for cover in all directions, fumbling dynamite sticks like children with burning potatoes in their hands. The lights were doused, the sentries fired off a few rounds in the air, not knowing who or what was on the beach, and a port security detachment of marines shoved off to drive the Japanese back into the hills.

It had been a close call. One round might have set off an explosion that would have killed or injured dozens, ruined the port, leveled the village, wrecked the LCI and the lighters, and disintegrated one funny old dynamite barge. What almost none there knew was that the explosion of the barge's cargo would also have destroyed what little was left of the third modern battleship built for the United States Navy. It was the U.S.S. *Oregon* (BB-3), once the most modern, proudest, finest, and most successful warship in the American service.

Forty-six years before, a sleek, trim man-of-war had astounded the world and filled the hearts of Americans with great pride by making a record-shattering, glorious dash around South America to join the American battle fleet in time to meet the Spanish fleet at Santiago de Cuba. The *Oregon* had steamed 14,500 miles in sixty-six days, sometimes coaling at sea, never stopping her engines for overhaul or repair. In doing so, she had had to elude Span-

ish torpedo boats searching for her and, in Caribbean waters, to avoid the entire fleet of Adm. Pascual Cervera y
Topete, who would have delighted in the opportunity to
chop up a single American battleship.

For the first time, a steam vessel had bested the record of the clipper ships in "rounding the Horn," and authorities would not only remark on the newly realized sea-
keeping capacity of a ship like the *Oregon,* but also would
and did remark: "There should have been a canal across
the Isthmus of Panama. It should have been possible to
bring the *Oregon* to the East Coast's defense even faster
and without sailing her around the whole of South
America."

On Sunday morning, July 3, 1898, after a blockade
of a month, Admiral Cervera steamed the Spanish fleet
out of the harbor of Santiago de Cuba to its destruction
and into history. The American battleships were waiting,
but only the *Oregon* had boilers lighted off and all main
machinery in operation. It was the *Oregon* that overhauled
and brought to bay the last and fastest of the Spanish
warships; it was the *Oregon* whose thirteen-inch guns
fired the last shots of the battle, driving the *Cristobal
Colon* into the beach. When the mustachioed bluejackets
of the other American ships saw the great white bow wave
of the *Oregon* looming up on them as the swift battleship
passed their slower vessels, her thirteen-inch and eight-
inch guns flinging shells furiously in all directions at the
fleeing Spanish battlewagons ahead and the desperately
maneuvering Spanish destroyers astern, the men rose
to the rails and shouted to each other, "There goes the
*Oregon* like a bulldog with a bone in her teeth!"

It might have been more fitting if the old battleship
had been blown to pieces under enemy fire at Guam instead of reaching the ignominious end she finally met.
But that demise and the glory of a brave ship that served
the United States Navy in three wars and for over fifty
years form the story of *McKinley's Bulldog: The Battleship* Oregon.

# 1

# The ABCD Navy

During the Civil War, the Union had built the finest, fastest, most powerful warships afloat. By 1880, the United States Navy had ceased to exist as a practical fighting force. Any one of several South American navies could have blown it to splinters—yes, splinters, for eighteen years after the *Monitor* stalemated the *Merrimac* (more properly the ram C.S.S. *Virginia*), only four American warships had iron hulls. The pattern of hurriedly and painfully achieved American military prowess, followed by public indifference and inevitable decay, had begun.

The Union navy once had seven hundred ships. It introduced armored combat vessels and proved their value under fire. It had perfected the rifled gun barrel, which fired projectiles farther and truer than the old smoothbore could toss a cannon ball, thus making possible modern gunnery ashore as well as afloat. The revolving gun turret, which could instantly make a protected gun a bow-chaser or a stern-chaser or a port or starboard broadsider at the whim of a commander and the turning of a steam-propelled table, was another Yankee innovation that should have made every wooden-hulled broadside ship-of-the-line obsolete. It really did, but conservative naval authorities were unable to realize that fact. During the war, the navy had introduced steam warships without sail rigging, yet steam warships constructed twenty-five years later would carry a full sail rig. After all, "machinery is unreliable (as well as dirty)," "coal is expensive," and "wooden ships make iron men."

Not only had the United States Navy been the first in the world to build a steamship, but it also had been the first to build one equipped with the screw propeller, which eliminated the cumbersome, vulnerable, speed-reducing side or stern paddles. And the U.S.S. *Wampanoag,* completed just after the Civil War, had been the fastest ship in the world. She had made nearly eighteen knots and, for the first time, a machinery-propelled vessel could outstrip the fastest clipper afloat.

And then the understandable antiwar feeling after the end of hostilities, the complacency of the inward-expanding continental power, and the indifference and shortsightedness of the Congress and the American people scuttled the navy. In 1881, the Royal Navy had more than 400 vessels on the active list, of which 56 were modern armored ships. The Japanese navy, which had purchased its first warship from the American government as late as 1866, had 5 new armored warships in a fleet of 19 fine vessels. The United States could "boast" a navy of all of 26 ships. Four of the smallest just happened to have iron hulls; the rest were wooden coffins. Up and down the East Coast, thanks to a foolish pork barrel policy, iron vessels had been "under construction" since 1865. In reality, they were obsolete rust piles. The entire American navy of 1880 could not have survived combat with one British predreadnought or the navy of Chile, let alone Spain.

The great energies of the United States were directed inward and westward for most of the last half of the nineteenth century. After the French fiasco in Mexico, Europe seemed quite willing to leave the Americas alone. There were enough spoils to be gathered in Africa and Asia. In addition, the growing continental rivalries among France, Germany, and Russia forced these nations to neglect, for the most part, the giant nation with a child's strength awakening across the Atlantic. And Britannia ruled the waves. Britain, although tempted to interfere in the Civil War on the side of the South and in the name of King Cotton, had nevertheless remained neutral, unable morally to support a nation of slave owners regardless of the economic advantages.

The Monroe Doctrine was in effect, but the United States was totally unable to enforce it without a significant fleet. It was the tacit support of the Royal Navy that prevented foreign incursions into the Western Hemisphere. The American payment for this support and cooperation was the existence of the Dominion of Canada. United States expansion remained south of the Canadian border, and European territorial ambitions were diverted by the British fleet.

In the 1870s and 1880s, it was inconceivable for most Americans that their nation might one day be a world power. Except for the possibility of expansion into the Caribbean, there was no thought of overseas colonial growth. After all, the United States was an importer of people, not an exporter. European immigrants were pouring into the Eastern cities at a rate unparalleled in the history of mankind. A great migration was taking place to fill up and develop a seemingly empty land whose native inhabitants were to have no say in determining the nature of the change and growth.

Furthermore, Americans looked back to the ideals

of the founding fathers especially as the centennial of the nation approached and passed. The United States had long opposed the concept of standing armies and had made its military particularly weak and peculiarly subject to civilian control, at least in the view of most other nations. Military and naval forces were to be defensive forces. The militia, lightly trained but available, could be mobilized in time of war, and the professionals would quickly bring its training up to date. Since a navy need only defend the coasts, no deep draught, high fuel-capacity vessels were necessary. Slowly, in the final decades of the nineteenth century, American attitudes began to change. The frontier was closing. The nation had reached its continental limits. The oceans were the new frontier. Trade and communication with Europe and Asia became increasingly more significant. Imperceptibly but steadily, the notion grew that the United States might have to be prepared to protect its own lines of communication and trade routes. The concept of defense might thus include control, not only of the immediate coastal waters, but even of far-flung sea lanes.

In the decade prior to the war with Spain, the fighting ships of the world were categorized as battleships, armored cruisers, protected cruisers, unprotected cruisers, destroyers, torpedo boats, monitors, gunboats, and dispatch boats. The battleship was indeed the queen of battle, and the navies of the world were rated according to the number of such vessels they could muster. Battleships then were great floating gun platforms of up to 15,000 tons displacement, with wrought iron or steel armor up to twenty-four inches thick. They mounted a mixed bag of guns from main battery thirteen-inchers down to one pounder rapid-fires. Optics and range finding were still somewhat primitive, and smokeless powder was just finding acceptance (the United States fleet at Santiago would fire old-style brown powder; the Spanish would have new smokeless), and so the value of long-range batteries was considered limited. Better to have faster firing, smaller caliber guns for poor visibility and close-in fighting, as well as Long Toms for long-range battleship encounters, chases, and shore bombardments. Battlewagons were not fast, eighteen knots maximum, but they were not supposed to run. They were heavyweights built to stand and fight.

Before Alfred Thayer Mahan explained and popularized the basic tenets of sea power, the battleships seemed to many Americans a totally aggressive weapon. But we saw ourselves as a peace-loving people minding our own business behind the comfortable walls of two vast oceans. (All we nonaggressive Americans had done in the nineteenth century was to conquer most of the world's third-largest continent.) In reality, American business had become worldwide, and no port on the globe did not regularly see the American flag on the staffs and trucks of a vast merchant marine peddling the enormous surplus of goods pouring from the factories of New York and New England. An American battle fleet was inevitable. Whether it was to be adequate was another question.

After battleships, in naval ratings, came the fast, twenty-four-knot armored cruisers, which were much like the heavy cruisers of World War II vintage. The cruisers of the 1890s had some armor but much less than the battleships had. The main battery consisted of eight eight-inch or six-inch guns, and the usual host of smaller calibers and rapid-fire guns was also present. The armored cruiser could steam vast ranges, scout the enemy, hit the commerce, outrun the wagons, and take on anything its size or smaller. In actual warfare, this class of vessel was almost always misemployed. Again and again, squadrons of armored cruisers wound up being forced to slug it out with the heavily armored battleships until the inevitable destruction of the former occurred.

Whereas the armored cruisers displaced a wide range of tonnages and sometimes displaced as much as a battleship, the protected cruisers seldom displaced more than 5,000 tons. Along with the unprotected cruisers, they formed a class roughly equivalent in function to the light cruiser of World War II. Protected cruisers had an armored deck for protection against high trajectory fire but no side armor for broadside or torpedo fire. They made up to twenty knots and had a limited cruising range. When the American navy was rebuilding in the 1880s, these ships were the darlings of compromise. Their lack of cruising range made them defensive, while their single or twin eight-inch or six-inch rifles along with other smaller weapons appeared formidable and comforting.

Unprotected cruisers were not much smaller than protected cruisers, but they had no armored deck. For safety against shellfire, they depended on compartmentation and on coal bunkers placed around the vitals of the ship. (What was supposed to protect the ship that had to fight after heavy steaming and before recoaling?) The largest guns that unprotected cruisers carried were five-inchers. Unprotected cruisers as well as the heavier cruisers and even battleships carried torpedoes. This most dreaded naval weapon, of which more will be said later, made little sense on cruisers that would theoretically use it on battleships and other cruisers except that a cruiser made a suicidally large target at the 400-yard effective range of a Whitehead torpedo. The weapons made absolutely no sense on an eighteen-knot battleship.

Destroyers were a somewhat more natural home for torpedoes. This class of vessels was a rapidly evolving one. First had come the torpedo boat, which had been hailed as the great new naval weapon of the nineteenth century. Some naval authorities of the day thought this inexpensive craft, dubbed the "mosquito boat," had made battleships obsolete, and at least one major European power had temporarily halted battleship construction. It is the law of war, however, that every new weapon engenders its defense. Soon navies developed a class called torpedo boat destroyers. These sturdy little tykes seemed quite lethal in themselves, being armed with torpedo boat weapons and possessing high speed, so designers developed a class called destroyers of torpedo boat destroyers, which is not the easiest thing to say when maneuvering or changing station, so the term was shortened to destroyers. These ships could churn at thirty-five knots. Besides torpedoes, they carried small rapid-fires. They displaced only 400 tons and had an extremely limited range.

The torpedo boat from its inception in the nineteenth century through its demise in World War II was the most overrated weapon in modern military history. Not even the zeppelin was so overestimated. The torpedo itself, of course, was and is a most deadly and effective instrument of war, especially when launched by a submarine. After all, German submarines sank over 11 million tons of Allied shipping in World War I and over 14 million tons in World War II. The tin fish found its true home in the sub, not in its original carrier, the torpedo boat.

The torpedo itself developed from the mine, a most effective passive weapon and the first to be called a torpedo. In fact, the torpedoes that Farragut was "damning" at Mobile Bay were actually such mines. Then came spar torpedoes, which were basically mines on the end of forty-foot spars projecting ten feet under water from vessels of the Royal Navy. These weapons were charged with gun cotton and electrically detonated from within the ship. The point of it all was to hit an enemy vessel at or below the waterline, and it was damned silly to have to throw one whole ship at another to achieve the shot. The self-propelled torpedo finally arrived on the naval scene in 1866 through the genius of an English engineer, Robert Whitehead. His torpedo was cigar shaped, measuring eleven feet in length and fourteen inches in diameter. It weighed 300 pounds and ran on compressed air. Almost every naval power in the world took an interest in and bought Whitehead torpedoes—except the United States.

In 1891, off the coast of Chile, the torpedo achieved a spectacular success that shook the naval world. The British torpedo boat *Lynch,* which had gotten involved in a Chilean revolt, torpedoed and sank the armored ship

*Bianco Encalada* with a fourteen-incher fired at a range
of a hundred yards. The blast knocked the skipper of the
*Bianco Encalada* into the sea. The reaction to the torpedo's dramatic success was similar to the reaction in world
naval circles in 1967 when Russian-built Egyptian-
manned, Komar-class patrol boats sank the Israeli destroyer *Elath* from over the horizon, at a distance of
twenty to twenty-five miles, with Styx surface-to-surface
missiles. Authorities began to take a second look at the
defenses of expensive aircraft carriers and cruisers. In
1891, however, the point much ignored in the ensuing dis-
cussions was that a single hostile torpedo boat had no
business being allowed within 1,000, let alone 100, yards
of an ironclad. When in 1896 the Austrian naval officer
Ludwig Obry invented the gyroscope and thus perfected
the stabilization of the torpedo, the naval world shook
again.

The torpedo boat itself would prove to be no match
for the destroyer, rapid-fire guns, and the electric search-
light. Nevertheless, in 1890, when the American navy finally got its first torpedo boat into commission, there
were nearly 1,000 such ships in service throughout the
world.

Then there was that vessel that held a special place
of honor in the hearts of Americans in general and tradi-
tion-bound Yankee naval officers in particular, most of
whom were veterans of the great blockade of 1861–1865.
It was the monitor, of course.

John Ericsson's brilliant invention had probably done
more to save the Union than any other weapon of the Civil
War. On the morning of Saturday, March 8, 1862, the
*Merrimac,* rebuilt as the ironclad C.S.S. *Virginia,* steamed
out into Hampton Roads and destroyed the wooden *Cumberland* and the grand old frigate *Congress.* It thus appeared that ironplated ships could destroy wooden vessels
at will. The Union blockade was an almost totally wooden
one, and in a few days it apparently would be reduced to a
paper one. The next day "the cheese box on a raft," the

*Monitor*—a low-freeboard, mastless, ironplated gun platform with two heavy cannon in a revolving steam turret
—fought the *Virginia* to a standoff and caused the larger
vessel to retreat. Northern despair turned to exultation
and, under Ericsson's supervision, the shipyards of the
North churned out cheap, quickly built monitors that were
double turreted and more seaworthy than the original
model.

The original *Monitor* foundered off Cape Hatteras
in a fierce gale on December 31, 1862, causing the loss of
sixteen lives. What was wrong with the first monitor was
wrong with all subsequent versions. Their dangerously
low reserve buoyancy, less than 20 percent, made them
death traps. Other armored warships at that time were
expected to have at least 80 percent reserve buoyancy. In
other words, such a ship would remain floating even if it
were 80 percent filled with water. But a monitor would
sink if water filled only a fifth of it. A monitor's low freeboard, only 1½ to 2 feet (about what a respectable row-
boat has), made the monitor an almost nonexistent target but also prevented the turret guns from firing in any
kind of seaway. In other words, the monitor was a great
coastal defense vessel and was used as such by other navies through World War II. To haul these slow, ungainly
ships around the world or to try to incorporate them into
a battle fleet—as Adm. William T. Sampson tried to do
against the Spanish—was as foolish as using elephants
against tanks. Yet the emotional attachment to the class
of ships that had saved the Union blockade at Hampton
Roads, at Charleston, and even at Mobile Bay was so strong
that, as late as 1886, Congress approved the completion
of the *Amphitrite, Monadnock, Puritan,* and *Terror,* double turret monitors planned at the close of the Civil War.
These ships were all iron and filled with modern machinery, but they were still monitors. The navy, like the
French in 1940, was still fighting the previous war.

Other vessels in the fleets of the last quarter of the
nineteenth century were the lightly armed and very ne-

cessary dispatch boats; essentially swift yachts, which
served as communicators between and among fleets and
bases; and the ubiquitous gunboats, primarily riverine
craft and blockaders displacing around 1,000 tons or less
and heavily armed with four-inch or even six-inch rapid-
fire guns.

The rapid evolution of naval weaponry in the late
1800s forced the United States to make a basic decision
concerning goals. Should the nation protect its commerce,
continue to enforce the Monroe Doctrine regardless of
British support, defend two vast coastlines, and justify
the growing self-image of Americans as a people whose
"manifest destiny" would take them, rightly or wrongly,
but seemingly inevitably, into the realm of imperialism
and the world of international power politics? If so, then
these new instruments of war, these swift and deadly
iron boxes of power, were the costly temptations without
which greatness and prestige could not come into being.
The weapons would have to be built or bought with money
that could have fed and housed and clothed and educated
millions of immigrant children in the slums of New York
and Chicago, millions of white and black children of the
American rural poor, and the entire Indian nations of the
West. The nation chose warships, and social services languished. But twentieth century America as we know her
would not have existed or exerted her mighty influence
on our days and our fathers' days if the nation had not,
after great soul-searching, said "yea" to power.

It all began with the letters ABCD and a congressional act of March 3, 1883. Congress provided for four
new steel-hulled vessels of American design. They were
the cruisers *Atlanta, Boston,* and *Chicago* and the dispatch boat *Dolphin.* The four ships became known as the
ABCD "fleet," or the "White Squadron." The vessels
were provided with a full sail rig and had many short-
comings in design. Nevertheless, they were American
made, and they became the proving ground for all subse-

quent modern naval construction. In 1885, Congress authorized two more cruisers, *Newark* and *Charleston,* and two gunboats, *Yorktown* and *Petrel.* We were on our way.

However, cruisers, like submarines in the later world wars, were primarily for raiding commerce. Monitors and other gunboats were for coast defense and riverine warfare. Only battleships could meet an enemy battle fleet on the high seas and defeat it before it reached the American coast. After all, in the War of 1812 the British had burned American seaboard cities at will. Neither the brilliant American single ship victories over British frigates nor the very effective privateering could prevent the burning of Washington or win the war.

The act of 1886 that provided for the completion of the four monitors also authorized the first two truly successful modern warships built in the United States. They were officially designated as second class battleships. They took nine years to build and were not commissioned until 1895. American steel mills took three years to produce the required amount of nickel steel. The first of the battleships was the *Texas,* which was built from English plans. The second, of completely American design, had a brief career of only two and a half years after commissioning, but she was long remembered. She was named the *Maine.*

Captain Alfred Thayer Mahan's *The Influence of Sea Power upon History. 1660–1783* was published in May, 1890, after his lectures to the Naval War College—upon which the book was based—had already begun to have an effect on naval officers, expansionist politicians, and defense-minded government officials. The Secretary of the Navy in the Harrison administration (1889–93), Benjamin F. Tracy, became a disciple of Mahan. Like the military philosopher, he believed that a strong navy would exempt this country from war. If war did come, however, it would have to be fought with the fleet in being; there would be no time for new construction. Tracy was right, at least in regard to the forthcoming war with Spain, if not to subsequent conflicts. We are back to his viewpoint again today.

Tracy was helped by an event known as the Samoa Crisis. On March 15, 1889, a squadron of German warships, three antiquated American cruisers, and the H.M.S. *Calliope* lay at anchor in the middle of Apin Harbor of the island of Upolu in the Samoan group. The crews were at battle stations, with the superior German naval force about to invalidate the three way Samoan Agreement. The Germans had bombarded Apia and were preparing to make the islands a German possession—over the bodies of the crews of the inferior American and British forces. The skies darkened, the winds and seas rose in fury, and an unprecedented hurricane smashed the warships, tossing them against each other like matchsticks and heaving them up on reefs and rocks. The German ambitions were shipwrecked, but the American squadron also was ruined. Only the *Calliope,* with steam up in new engines, was able to beat her way out of the coral vise and into open sea. The incident showed Americans what sea power could do and what it had not done. A second-class, underpowered, undergunned navy was clearly no navy at all. The Samoan Crisis made the American public sea-conscious. The dispute was finally settled on June 14, 1889, when a tripartite protectorate over the islands was arranged. German ambitions had been thwarted, but by an act of God and not by the power of the United States Navy.

On June 30, 1890, the Republican administration pushed through a congressional act that provided for three battleships. They were called "seagoing coastal battleships" —a term for all seasons. "Seagoing" pleased the "Big Navy" expansionists, and "coastal" appealed to those who valued economy and defensive strategy. The battleships would displace about 10,000 tons each. The armor belt would be eighteen inches thick. Armament would consist of a main battery of four thirteen-inch guns and secondary batteries of eight-inch and six-inch guns. Unfortunately, the "coastal" compromise limited the speed to a little over sixteen knots and gave the ships coal capacity for a cruising range of less than 5,000 miles. Still, these ships could and would form the nucleus of the new battle fleet and indeed prove to be a lot more "seagoing" than "coastal."

Two of the new ships were built in Philadelphia and named *Indiana* and *Massachusetts*. The third contract was awarded to two energetic San Francisco shipbuilders, Irving M. Scott and Henry Scott of the Union Iron Works. Their ship would be named *Oregon*.

This *Oregon* would not be the first *Oregon* in the United States Navy. Number one was a brig of 187 tons, purchased in 1841 and used by Lt. Charles Wilkes, U.S.N., to survey the Columbia River. She was then sailed around the Cape of Good Hope to the east coast of the United States and sold in 1845. The second *Oregon* was a double-turret monitor, or would have been one had she ever been finished. Laid down in the Boston Navy Yard in 1864, she was to have two pairs of heavy guns mounted on fifteen-inch armored turrets. When the Civil War ended, work was halted, and she rotted and rusted for nineteen years as part of the "paper fleet." The Navy Department mercifully had the junk pile broken up in 1884.

No, the new *Oregon* would not be the first of her name, but she would prove to be the first of the new navy. At her birth, she would be the largest, toughest, most powerful American fighting ship built to that date.

# 2

# The Launching: "Like Crested Pallus Armed"

The shoring, cutting, hauling, heaving, hammering, riveting, and pounding had taken two years. Now the unchristened hull sat in her cradle and waited for her first caress from the element that would be her home for as long as she existed. Her keel had been laid on November 19, 1891, at San Francisco's Union Iron Works, then only six years old. Now, almost two years later, she was ready for launching. All of San Francisco was ready too.

The dawn of Thursday, October 26, 1893, was dull, with the not-unusual fog bank hovering over San Francisco Harbor. The sun beyond the layers of clouds made its presence known slowly but surely, as if it too did not wish to miss the gala event. By eleven-thirty, it would break through and splash a memorable scene with a brimming pot of golden light.

The *Oregon* sat on her slippery chute with her rudder lashed fore and aft like the blade of a cutting spade. Long before dawn, her decks swarmed with mechanics, dockyard workers, riggers, and nervous foremen putting on the finishing touches. The debutant *Oregon* looked like a plump girl of the fashionable Lillian Russell configuration wearing a bathing suit of bright red from her keel to the waterline and more somber lead gray above, except for the two turrets and the barbettes, which had also been given a coat of flaming red in honor of the occasion.

Alas, there had been a social dispute concerning the launching. Several young Oregon ladies, all daughters of prominent men, had vied for the honor of breaking the traditional bottle of wine over the bow of the new vessel and giving her her name. Fortunately, the fracas had been settled without bloodshed. Two young ladies would share the honor. Miss Daisy Ainsworth, representing the state of Oregon, would have the privilege of pressing a button commencing a Rube Goldberg series of causes and effects that supposedly would send a bottle of California (of course) champagne crashing against the bow of the vessel. At the same moment, Miss Eugenia Shelby, representing the city of Portland, would press her own electric button. It would cause a small guillotine to drop and sever a cord holding twenty-two five-pound weights in position. The weights would pound against the dog shores securing the ship in position and theoretically release the new princess of the seas and send her on her way. It was all to happen at precisely 11:45 A.M. Miss Ruth Dolph, daughter of Sen. Joseph Norton Dolph of Oregon, had been designated by Secretary of the Navy Hilary Abner Herbert to represent the service at the christening, but she chose not to attend, possibly because there was nothing left for her to do.

The customary christening platform had been built before the bow of the ship and draped with swirls and criss crosses of red, white, and blue bunting. A panoply of flags, banners, and pennants canopied the platform with a Gothic arch of color. On the platform and directly under the overhang of the bow stood a table holding some of the gimcracks of electric launching: the little guillotine with its sharp knife resting on a protecting block above the cord. Behind this machine stood a small gold-framed oil painting of Mount Hood, Oregon. A tiny card stuck into one corner of the frame was inscribed, "To the battle ship Oregon, compliments of Miss Eugenia Shelby." The picture was the first gift the *Oregon* would receive. There were many more to come, most more expensive, but none more touching. To the left of the painting was a small box surmounted with a photo of the *Oregon* and containing the electric signaling device that was to notify the platform guests when all was in readiness below. The signal buttons for the young ladies were there too. The bottle of champagne was hanging from the railing of the platform above the table, ready for the christening.

San Franciscans had been gathering from the early hours of the morning. Those fortunate enough to have tickets to enter the shipyard and perhaps sit in the stands could afford to arrive later, but the ordinary people of the city came early. A man named Benjamin Conger, shoved by the crowd, had his toes crushed by a cable car on his way to the launching. Kentucky Street, which led down to the shipyard, was aswarm with humanity on foot or in hacks. Men and women began to line the shore for half a mile below the *Oregon*'s berth, and the narrow street to the gate of the Union Iron Works was dangerously jammed and blocked by ten that morning. Fortunately, company officials threw open four gates to admit the general throng. This act caused a wild, trampling stampede for points of vantage near the ship's cradle. Boys and young men, like flies on meat, began to climb along the timbers of the stocks fifty feet above the superstructure of the ship. Shipyard guards had to force men back from beneath the very ways. The people perched and waited like patient gulls.

The roofs of the nearby Arctic Oil Works were filled with men and women, and some enterprising boys had obtained a long ladder to climb to the top of the tallest tank in the ironworks. Theirs was indeed a bird's-eye view.

In Mission Bay an immense fleet of vessels had congregated to honor the *Oregon*. In fact, never before had so many ships and craft gathered there. "Is there any room left for the launching?" many worried officials began to wonder. Giant ferry steamers, loaded to the guard rails with thousands of people, elbowed into the harbor. The excursion steamer *Ukiah* dangerously tested her passenger capacity; so did the stern-wheeler *Caroline*. Hundreds of men, women, and children clung to saucy-looking cutters, swift-sailing yachts, tugs, steam launches, punts, racing shells, and rowboats, all of which formed a crescent-shaped armada around the ironworks. The steamer *Walla Walla*, in the big dry dock at the ironworks, was full-rigged with people, some three thousand having scampered aboard and covered every inch of deck, superstructure, mast, and spar.

Foreign vessels tied up nearby displayed all the bunting and flags they could break out. The big Norwegian ship *Bredablik*, at Long Wharf, was a veritable Christmas tree of flags. In fact, every single harbor craft streamed with patriotic banners. Voices and whistles and cannon were ready to mark a great day for Uncle Sam and the United States Navy as well as California and San Francisco!

The United States Quartermaster's boat *General McDowell* hove into sight with the Presidio band aboard playing "Hail Columbia." Near the band stood the Presidio's commanding officer, Gen. Thomas Howard Ruger, and his staff, all decked out in their splendid full-dress blues with gold epaulets. The steam launch *Rockaway* shoved off from Mission Pier at 10:30 with a deckload of Union Iron Works officials, directors, and guests. The naval officers from Mare Island steamed down aboard the tug *Monarch*, while other government officials and their ladies rode on the revenue cutters *Corwin* and *MacArthur*.

The tugs *Fearless, Vigilant, Active, Sea Queen,* and *Rescue,* which had been chartered by clubs and private parties, chugged as close to the official boats as they could get.

The big steamer *Bay City* carried hundreds of passengers to the scene of the launch for fifty cents a head. Several small steamers, including *Pride of the River,* had been chartered by enterprising speculators, who had sold passage to the launching for various fares and were reaping small fortunes.

Then the most important vessels of the celebration fleet hove into view. First came the fire tug carrying California governor, Henry Harrison Markham, San Francisco's mayor, Ellert, the city commissioners, and other officials. The tug was named the *Governor Markham,* of course. Gov. Markham had invited Gov. Sylvester Pennoyer of Oregon to attend the launching with him, but the latter official had declined. The snub caused the San Francisco *Chronicle* to complain that "had the battle ship been forwarded to East Portland and slid into the Williamette [*sic*] he might have consented to shed the lustre of his presence on the scene." Instead, Gov. Pennoyer had delegated Gen. G. Compton (Oregon Militia) of Portland as his proxy. The general would be one of the platform guests.

Following close astern of the *Governor Markham* was the red-stacked tug *Sea King.* Aboard were navy yard Comdnt. Captain Henry L. Howison, U.S.N.; his staff; and the Mare Island Marine Band. Within three years, Captain Howison would place the *Oregon* in commission on the Pacific station. From July, 1896, through March, 1897, he would serve as her first commanding officer.

By eleven-thirty, the crowd in the ironworks, along the beaches, in the overlooking buildings, and in the harbor was estimated at more than 100,000 people. It was indeed a great day for the navy, San Francisco, and the Eastman Kodak Company, whose new box cameras were everywhere in sight. When the sun broke to the masthead of the sky, the "Kodak fiends" shouted with joy and began snapping.

With the arrival of the platform guests, all but the last props and shores had been removed and the ways liberally slushed with tallow. The ship rested in her cradle. Each important guest was met and escorted to the platform by Irving M. Scott. The first to mount the ladder was General Ruger, whose full-dress blues and gold-tasseled sword had survived the voyage across the bay in fine style. He was followed by his staff officers, Colonel Moule, Colonel Miles, and Major Egan. Then up went General Compton in a cocked hat and sword, followed—at a respectable distance behind the dangling weapon—by Judge W. B. Gilbert of the circuit court.

Other distinguished visitors scampered aloft. Then came a navy band which quickly formed a circle, and played "The Star-Spangled Banner," followed by "A Home on the Rolling Deep" and other nautical and patriotic airs. In the middle of a number, the heroines of the day appeared, surrounded by a host of relatives, friends, and male admirers. Miss Ainsworth, a petite girl wearing a snug-fitting ankle-length red dress and clutching a bunch of lilies, was so eagerly aided in her ascent that she was practically hoisted aloft like a red ensign climbing to the main truck. Next came Miss Shelby, oppositely colored in a navy blue hat and a dress of the same color, with a large bunch of chrysanthemums on her ample, heaving bosom. She, too, with a little more effort on the part of the willing haulers, soon flew aloft.

The gallant General Compton, exerting the privilege of rank, took the ladies in tow immediately and began to initiate them into the mysteries of ship launching. He explained the electric appliances at great length and assured the ladies of their safety from electrocution. They listened attentively as he told them how many pounds of pressure per square inch they should bring to bear on the buttons. The girls looked at the buttons and then at the

great iron ship, not believing for one moment that they
would actually be able to move that enormous hulk even
a fraction of an inch. Miss Shelby was particularly concerned lest the bottle fail to break. Would they have to
haul the vessel back into the cradle and up the ways to
launch it again? Would she be held accountable?

More visitors arrived and soon the platform was filled,
about half of those present being ladies. Irving M. Scott
and Henry Scott piloted the guests around the platform,
pointing out details of the ship and the ironworks. Irving
M. Scott lectured to the assemblage on the cost, the construction, and the promise of the *Oregon*:

> When fitted out, the ship will have cost the United
> States Government well over $4,000,000. Her displace-
> ment loaded will be 10,288 tons. The *Oregon,* like her
> sisters, was designed with a view of meeting in battle
> vessels carrying the heaviest guns and armor. She was
> designed after a careful study of the vessels of other
> powers, and with a view to being operated upon the
> coasts of America. The *Oregon* is a vessel of great
> fighting power united with adequate protection in the
> shape of high-resisting armor. Her draught is suffi-
> ciently small to enable her to be operated in the shal-
> low waters of the American coast.
>
> The following are the principal features of the
> *Oregon*: Length on the water line, 348 feet; beam,
> extreme, 69¼ feet; draught, forward and aft, 24 feet;
> eventual displacement, 10,200 tons; designed maximum
> speed, 16.2 knots; sustained sea speed, 15 knots.[1]

Now it was the turn of Henry Scott to play Cicero
to the guests. He explained how the large vessel was held
in check and how she would be set free. One lady asked,
"Do you plan on anyone being killed in the launching?"
to which Scott replied in the negative. Another timid
lady wanted to know if the platform was attached to the
ship and whether it would be carried along down the ways.
She too was reassured. Meanwhile, the band sawed on
lustily as the hammers clicked and thumped away on the
ways below. It was time to start the ceremony.

First there was an original poem to be read. It had been written by one Samuel L. Simpson of Astoria, Oreg., in twelve stanzas and entitled, naturally enough, "The Launching of the Oregon." The poem had been telegraphed down to San Francisco by the board of trade of Astoria, along with the highest literary recommendations. The audience bared their heads in reverence as Mrs. M. J. Kinney of San Rafael hurled the lines at the defenseless vessel:

Oh, ship, like crested Pallas armed,
Oh, bride, the hoary god hath charmed....[2]

The *Oregon* began to creak in her cradle and seemed to tug at the dog shores holding her.

The poem was loudly cheered upon its conclusion. Irving M. Scott then introduced the Reverend C. O. Brown of the First Congregationalist Church of San Francisco, who invoked the blessings of the Almighty in a short but moving prayer. The Reverend Mr. Brown had intended to speak at length, but a large bumblebee, attracted by the impressive floral arrangements on the platform, had somewhat nearsightedly attempted to light on the good pastor's upturned nose. Brown quickly shouted "Amen!" and retreated to the rear of the platform, waving his hat in front of him.

An electrician came forward to put the electric buttons in their proper places and set the guillotine. The ladies of the electric launching were ushered to their places before the table, and General Compton covered the rear to make sure they manned their guns and did not miss their cues. More flowers were gallantly proffered: to Miss Daisy was given a large bunch of yellow chrysanthemums, while Miss Eugenia received an enormous bouquet of red roses.

The two Scotts held the positions between the table and the bow, where they could communicate with the man in charge of the men below. High up on the bow of the ponderous hull stood the riggers who were to take the ride down into the bay. Still higher up perched a vast audience of men and boys, clinging with tooth and nail to the timbers and waiting for the signal.

The exhausted band had stopped for lack of wind, and no sound was heard but the blows of hammers. Nearer and nearer came the thumps that were placing more responsibility on the dog shores. Shore after shore dropped with a crash, and then the perspiring workmen appeared under the bow. It was almost 11:45, the prescribed time for the launching, but there still remained a few blocks to clear away.

They were stubborn ones that refused to yield to hammer alone. Chisels were brought and, splinter by splinter, the forward keel blocks were chipped and hacked. As the last one gave way, the hull settled squarely on the ways, and the road to the sea was clear. Nothing remained but for the little guillotine to do its work.

"Are you ready below?" yelled Irving Scott.

The answer came with a click, and the word "Ready" showed in the electric box in front of Miss Ainsworth. With a steady hand, she pressed the button, and the keen-edged knife fell on the restraining rope. For a moment, the ship sat motionless, and the great throng watched for the first sign of life. Slowly the *Oregon* felt her weight and started. With never a quiver or jar, she moved off down the incline, but there was something amiss. The bottle of champagne still hung on its hook. Miss Shelby pressed away at her button, but the bottle refused to budge. The *Oregon* was about to escape this part of the ceremony and would have but for the prompt action of Henry Scott.

Just before the ship had traveled beyond reach, he leaped to the rail of the platform, grabbed the bottle from its hook, and dashed it against the bow of the ship.

"I name thee *Oregon*," murmured Miss Daisy Ainsworth as the huge hulk started down the toboggan ride, and a wild, glad cheer went up from more than 100,000 throats.

On the stroke of 12:00, the biggest iron battleship of them all glided gently into the waters of the bay. Flags and banners floated fore and aft, and her red bow was wet with the baptismal wine. A crash and a splash marked the instant that the ship rode down to the sea and jammed her stern into the mud flats—properly launched, named, and baptized.

The huge wave that ran ahead of the launch spoiled the view of those standing on the shore. The miniature tsunami rolled up the beach and rose to the waists of those in the front rank. There was a frantic rush to escape, but the jumbled mass of people, hacks, and peanut wagons in the background cut off the only way to safety.

Several people were carried off their feet and tumbled about in the mud by the playful tidal wave, and some were badly bruised. One William P. Vaughn was washed into the bay, and, before he was rescued, a raft struck one of his legs and broke it. He was carried to the Receiving Hospital.

The *Oregon* entered the water stern first. The rudder was in place and had to be clamped so that it might act as a cutwater when the vessel was launched. This it did nicely, and the wave that was raised by the big battleship was white capped.

No one can tell beforehand just what any vessel will do when launched, but the *Oregon* had been figured to a nicety, and, with credit to its builders and launchers, behaved wonderfully well. The Union Iron Works people had learned by experience what practical workings were. They had made mistakes in the past and were evidently trying to profit from former failures to score future successes in both building and launching all kinds of vessels.

For a month past, a dredger had been at work deepening the offing where the war vessel was to enter the water. It was supposed by many that, in the first plunge, the *Oregon* might take a dive and stick in the mud. However, the moment the big hull commenced to move in the water, it proved buoyant as a cork. The ship was sustained by the heavy-timbered cradle until well afloat. Then mooring chains braked the cradle while the *Oregon,* powered by its momentum, continued forward and floated by itself.

The cradle blocks and wedges floated in one mass while the *Oregon* was brought to an anchorage less than 150 yards from the stocks she was built on. She was a pretty sight, this mammoth warship, the bright red paint on the turrets, sponson, and topsides glistening in bold relief in the strong sunlight, while the dark lead color of waterline and bilge showed just how much deeper the ship must go when the engines and the boilers and the armament would be mounted and the vessel coaled.

The noise that greeted the big fighter as she plunged into the water was something terrific: "Its like was never heard on the borders of the vast Pacific before." [3] The hoarse siren of the big steamer blended its notes with the shrill treble of the tiny steam launch, and the volume of sound seemed to shake the very hills that surround the bay. The excitement among the spectators on board the big fleet was tremendous. Men shouted and waved their hats and the ladies hurrahed and waved their handkerchiefs as the *Oregon* came to rest after her maiden plunge. Small boys in small boats were out in force and vied with the sturdy boatmen for the post of honor on the occasion. This post, of course, was as close to the ship's stern as possible. The daring mariners remained there until the ship began to move, and then there was a scurrying to get out of the way. Some succeeded, but a luckless few were caught by the big wave thrown up by the battleship as she rushed into the water, and several of the small craft were swamped. The occupants of the inundated boats were quickly rescued by their friends, and, except for a good ducking, no one was much the worse for the accident.

Hardly had the big ship become stationary after her plunge when she was surrounded by hundreds of the small craft, the occupants of which eagerly inscribed their names on her gray-painted sides. The immense fleet of vessels remained for a few minutes to gaze at the warship and then headed back for the city again.

Those who were on the *Oregon* when she slid down the ways were as follows: John Murray, foreman of the engineroom; James McKay, in charge of the fireroom and boilers; Thomas Longworth, in charge of the deck, machinery, and ventilation; A. Martin, foreman of the construction works; W. Donald, foreman of shipjoiners; Richard Sture, foreman of riggers; W. Telfer, foreman of shipsmiths; A. Donaldson, captain of the dry dock; and A. Smith, chief engineer, dry dock.

The knocking out of wedges and blocks—the task that allowed the *Oregon* to rest in the cradle directly on the shores—was performed by a gang of workmen under the supervison of James Dickie, superintendent of construction, and E. T. Morris, chief engineer of the works. Other officials actively engaged in the building of the vessel were George Dickie, manager of the works; Robert Forsyth, assistant manager; Hugo Frear, chief draughtsman; and R. Pengelly, foreman of shipwrights.

It had been a good show. All parties were truly satisfied—the navy, the builders, the officials, and, most of all, the people of San Francisco. Slowly, the crowds melted off the buildings, away from the beaches, and down from the ships tied up at the ironworks. Some of the last spectators came down the ladders of the new cruiser launched only a year before at the Union Iron Works and still being fitted out. Her name was the *Olympia*, and one day she would lead Dewey's squadron to glory and victory at Manila Bay. Two months after that, the *Oregon* would prove to be the key ship at the Battle of Santiago.

These two ships, launched a year apart in the same shipyard and made by the same builders, influenced American history and changed American destiny more than any other warships ever built, with the possible exceptions of Perry's *Niagara* on Lake Erie in 1813, Farragut's

*Hartford* at New Orleans and Mobile Bay, and Halsey's *Enterprise* during World War II.

The *Oregon* and the *Olympia,* waiting together that October day in 1893, would find their destiny less than five years later as instruments by which America won an empire and became an international power.

# 3

# At the Ready

The outfitting proceeded apace, but five years passed between keel and commission. The builders had to cast and turn and mount the guns, place and set the boilers and engines, and mount the armor plate. During both construction and outfitting, custom and regulation mandated continual government inspections.

The major problem was the shaping and installing of the plate, for only two American steel companies had begun to learn how to forge large quantities of armor to warship specifications. The Bethlehem Steel Corporation developed this capacity first, and the Carnegie Steel Corporation followed. In fact, the requirement for large amounts of armor plate for the United States Navy enormously increased the capacity and technical ability of the American steel industry.

Carnegie was awarded the armor plate contract for

the *Oregon*. However, before the company could begin to manufacture the armor, the all-important question of the shape of the plate had to be answered. One school of naval construction argued for vertical armor—that is, armor without much curvature and set perpendicularly. It was relatively easy to make and install. Of course, the steel companies were in favor of this design. A second school, which included most naval constructors, insisted on inclined armor, which was set at an angle that theoretically would help deflect projectiles. The vertical won out and Carnegie produced Harveyized (carbon hardened) steel plate. This armor failed its first tests against close-range large projectiles. But Secretary of the Navy Herbert reduced the specification requirements and accepted the armor in December, 1894.

Finally, the Scott brothers notified the Navy Department that the *Oregon* was nearing completion. The department appointed a board of officers as a trial board to see that the contractors had met every detail of the agreement under which the ship had been built. The board had to certify that the vessel was seaworthy and able to carry specified weights without undue strain, and—of particular importance to both contractor and government —that she could develop contract speed or better. A bonus clause in the original *Oregon* contract offered $25,000 for each quarter knot of additional speed beyond the fifteen-knot specification.

The trial board's endlessly detailed inspection would determine the acceptability of the ship. The holds, passages, magazines, storerooms, watertight bulkheads and doors, and all movable parts had to be inspected and ascertained acceptable and functioning properly both at sea and in port. The ship had to be run at varying speeds to check the engines, the consumption of coal, the steam pressure produced, and the amount of vibration. Also, the ship had to be steered in circles to locate helm angles and tactical diameter and to test-exercise the three steering systems: hydraulic, steam, and hand. Most important of all was the measured course run for the full-speed trial.

In May, 1896, the Navy Department ordered Rear Adm. L. A. Beardslee, U.S.N., to head up the trial board "in addition to his other duties" and among his assistants, prophetically, were Capt. Charles Edgar Clark, U.S.N., and Chief Engineer Robert W. Milligan, U.S.N. Clark did not then dream that he would command the *Oregon* only two years later in one of the most fateful sea actions in American history, the brilliant run around the Cape to join Sampson's battle fleet and route the Spanish at Santiago. Milligan would be in charge of the engineering spaces on that same epic voyage. More than to any other human beings, with the possible exception of the Scott brothers, the *Oregon* would owe her glory to these two naval officers. They would learn much about their future home in serving on the trial board for the U.S.S. *Oregon*.

Admiral Beardslee reluctantly commenced the additional duty. He was a busy man, and he shuddered at the potential paper work necessary in the "temporary additional duty" (TAD in modern naval terminology). Furthermore, the responsibilities were very great indeed.

The selection of a course for the full-speed trial was of great importance. The course had to be a thirty- or forty-mile straightaway in deep water not very far from the shore, fairly protected from the sea, and out of the track of tugs and sailing vessels. The board elected to use the Santa Barbara Channel, an almost ideal course that had been used in testing the *Olympia*, the *Monterey*, the *Charleston*, and other vessels. The channel extends between the southern coast of California and a group of four islands—Anacapa, Santa Cruz, Santa Rosa, and San Miguel—that lie parallel to the coast and some twenty to twenty-five miles distant from it, thus affording partial protection from southeast to southwest. The water is deep nearly to the shore, so that between Point Conception and Santa Barbara light—thirty-seven miles along

the coast—there is a straight east-and-west course of
thirty-one miles, at an average distance of four miles
from the beach, with a depth nowhere less than 100 fathoms. The coast, which consists of low foothills, included
many conspicuous and easily distinguishable marks, such
as lighthouses, windmills, and wharves. Furthermore, the
positions of these landmarks were accurately charted.
Thus, a navigator was able by cross bearings to know his
position at any part of the course.

To doubly assure the navigator, the United States
Coast Survey had planted, at intervals of about ten miles,
a number of pairs of tall stakes. The stakes of each pair
were a few hundred yards apart, and they were set on a
line at right angles to the east-and-west course. The distance from one pair of stakes to the next had been accurately measured, and all measurements were verified
before a trial was made. The stakes had been freshly whitewashed for the occasion so that they could easily be seen.
As a result of all these preparations, a ship running on
the course could readily determine its exact position. The
officer of the deck would watch the broad angle between
the stakes of one pair until, when the stakes were in line,
the angle disappeared. Then the officer prolonged this
line until it intersected the course of the ship.

On the morning of May 7, the inspection began. The
board, arrayed in overcoats (for it was a foggy and cold
California morning) mustered on a tug at the foot of
Market Street. The craft bore them over a very choppy
sea to the Union Iron Works, where the *Oregon* lay at
anchor. As the men drew alongside of her and gazed up
with some little awe at the high steel precipice they were
about to scale, their first sensation was one of littleness.
As fixed as a rock she lay, apparently in contempt of the
nasty little sea, which kept the tug dancing to such an extent that the most expert boat jumper among them wished
heartily that he were a better one. Their awe and dismay
were not sensibly diminished when, on stepping over the
side, they landed on an immense, wet, and considerably

lumbered-up deck. The *Oregon* had just returned from a builder's trial to adjust compasses, and her deck was a confusion of enormous chains, hawsers, blocks, windlasses, guns, capstans, and pumps. For a couple of hours, the board wandered in small groups over and around the ship, lost in her immensity, and lost absolutely when they assayed the intricate passages of "down below." When the men assembled to plan and organize their work, a universal air of depression was plainly manifest, for the three officers had begun to realize the magnitude of the task before them. They listened with great interest to the suggestions of the official inspectors, who had gotten on familiar terms with the monster. However, as Beardslee, Clark, and Milligan buckled down to their work, the depression wore off.

After a day spent in inspection, they met to compare notes, finding themselves quite capable of disputing vigorously. Each proved to his own satisfaction that he understood what he was talking about.

Having divided themselves into subcommittees, the board members donned working suits and took up their task. Clark dived into holds, magazines, and shellrooms, crawled through double bottoms, and climbed into military tops and turrets. Milligan, in turn, toured engineering spaces. Beardslee remained in charge on the bridge. The ship's medical officer, who had nothing strictly professional to do until someone tumbled down a hatch or got stuck in a narrow passage, armed himself with a Kodak and crawled around for views. Each diver, crawler, and climber was provided by Union Iron Works officials with a brand-new memorandum book in which were pages headed "Defects Observed." When the inspectors reassembled to compare notes, those pages were in nearly all cases blank. At the most, they bore brief memoranda followed by question marks, which meant "to be referred for discussion." Every time someone proposed the question "Does this conform with the contract?" the vote was unanimously "aye." The board members were duty bound to take nothing for granted, but they were not to assume that all was wrong until proved right. Beardslee was authorized to accept the reports of preceding inspectors: otherwise his work would have been endless, for he could not judge the tensile strength and elastic limit of the millions of pounds of steel, nor the weights and dimensions of the thousands of parts that had entered into the composition of the ship and were now covered over. The board had confidence in the builders' ability and character, which had been demonstrated by good and honest work in building the *Olympia*, the *Monterey*, and the *Charleston*—three ships that later sailed with Dewey to Manila.

The *Oregon* left San Francisco early on May 9, not making a straight run to Santa Barbara, but devoting much time to experimental work—stopping at full speed and backing, running with one engine or both, and steering by different methods. When she did reach Santa Barbara, on the afternoon of the tenth, the board had a very fair idea of her performance under quite a range of varying situations—all, however, in fair-weather conditions. Beardslee and Clark longed (officially) for a gale.

The experiments continued until the thirteenth, when the final speed and endurance trial was to have taken place. A stiff breeze and a heavy swell from the southeast made a postponement necessary in order to secure a fair trial, so that day was spent at anchor. Some of the men wrote up notes, some enjoyed the hospitalities of the country club of Santa Barbara, some indulged in the delightful drives for which Santa Barbara was noted, and some worked at inspecting the deep holds.

Several United States vessels had been detailed to the service of the board, including the coast survey steamers *Gedney* and *McArthur*, the fishing commission's steamer *Albatross*, and the Mare Island tug *Unadilla*. A vessel was anchored at each end of the thirty-mile course, and the rest were stationed at intervals of ten miles along the channel. These ships served a twofold purpose. In the first place, their officers used special instruments to ob-

serve the direction and strength of the tidal and current
flow during the trial and then corrected the speed record
to allow for the flow. In the second place, the ships served
as steering marks for the on-deck watch of the *Oregon*.
With the mast of an anchored vessel for a front sight and
the *Oregon*'s jackstaff for a rear one, the helmsman could
steer exactly.

At 7:00 A.M. on the 14th, Chief Engineer Robert
Forsyth, a Union Iron Works man who superintended the
engine department, reported all ready; and Irving M. Scott
gave the word, "Go!" The *Oregon* was to run thirty sea
miles to the westward, turn, and repeat to the eastward.

At 8:00 A.M., after a preliminary warming-up spin,
the *Oregon* dashed across the first range line at a 17-knot
gait. Passing Goleta Point, six miles beyond, she was going 17.5 knots (allowing for tidal correction, 17.34). The
joyful ship leaped forward. She had her head. Everything
was favorable. There was a light head swell that had no
effect upon the ship; the accompanying moderate head
wind gave her fires a good draft. It was a wonderful
and exciting spectacle. Imagine the momentum and the
pent-up energy of that ten-thousand-ton projectile with
a velocity of thirty feet per second! The mere humans
aboard were thrilled.

The run for the first thirty sea miles was at an average speed of over seventeen knots. As the *Oregon* neared
Point Conception, the conditions grew less favorable. The
head wind freshened, and the head swell increased considerably; the bow cut through instead of over, and the forward deck was afloat, which gave the board a chance to
observe its freedom from leaks. A sea crashed hard! The
jackstaff washed away, depriving the helmsman of his
rear sight.

The sea was pouring over the bows in green masses
and rushing aft in rivers, until, striking the foot of the
forward turret, it deluged with spray everyone stationed
there. Scott was comfortably seated under the lee of the
pilothouse, apparently as unconcerned as though he were

a passenger. As Beardslee, up to his eyes in business, was hurriedly passing Scott, the contractor detained the admiral a moment to chat about some matter of trifling importance. Beardslee, a man of nervous temperament, grew impatient. The unbroken train of successes on every trial of the ship had strongly biased him in favor of the *Oregon*. He dreaded that, at this crucial test, a journal might tear or something else go wrong. He was excited, and Scott noticed it.

"What's your hurry, Admiral? What are you excited about?" he asked.

"Great heavens, Mr. Scott," Beardslee answered, "why are *you not* excited? The breaking of a ten-cent bolt may cost you a hundred thousand dollars."

"Yes," retorted Scott, "I fully realize it; but *it isn't going to break. I know them all personally.*" Such sublime nerve could have been based only upon the utmost confidence in his own work.

However, after it was all over, Beardslee referred to this incident in correspondence with Scott, who replied, "Well, Admiral, I may have shown a smooth surface, but if you had only bored inside!"

The *Oregon* reached her western terminus some minutes ahead of schedule; so she ran a couple of miles farther before finally turning to port. The sea had by then increased, and the crew anticipated that when it got abeam they should have a heavy roll. They therefore braced themselves and hung on for support; but the *Oregon* fooled them. The roll was very slight, and there was not a moment when every gun aboard could not have been used effectively. The return to the eastward was but a repetition, except that the draft was inferior because the ship was running with the wind; the firemen were not so fresh; and the fires were therefore less bright. As a result, the speed fell off a little. The *Oregon* made her eastward run at an average of 16.49 knots, and the average for the entire sixty-two sea miles was 16.791 knots. This was the *Oregon*'s official record for four hours, and it earned her builders a $175,000 bonus.

In observing the speed, Beardslee had noticed early in the trial that the two patent logs did not agree. As the *Oregon* passed Goleta Point, they disagreed, not only with each other, but with the distance by range. The logs were promptly hauled in and put out of commission. Three groups of officers were stationed to observe the ranges— one group on the bow, one on the midship bridge, and one aft. When the whitewashed stakes came into line at the bow station, the officers there ordered, "Mark!" The midship station and the aft station repeated the procedure, and with every shout of "Mark!" the steam whistle gave a short, sharp blast. The exact time of each blast was recorded. This sequence of events was repeated at each station, and finally the figures were averaged out. If the mean of the times of the first and third blasts coincided with the time of the second, the correctness of the figures was confirmed. It always was, for plenty of drill had made the boys accurate. For a few hours, however, there was lively work. Sixteen and three-quarter knots per hour means about twenty-eight feet per second. The observing stations were only a little over a hundred feet apart; so the *Oregon* passed a station every four seconds. There was no time to make mistakes.

The board had no doubt as to the accuracy of the marking, but they were very glad of an additional and incontrovertible proof of speed: William R. Eckart, consulting engineer of the Union Iron Works, had contrived a very ingenious automatic device by which the steam of the second blast opened and immediately closed a shutter in a camera aimed shoreward. Each resulting photograph showed the whitewashed stakes in line.

After the speed test and the four-hour endurance trial, the *Oregon* was run another hour, slowing down by degrees, like a racehorse, to cool off. Then she steamed to her Santa Barbara anchorage, where Beardslee telegraphed the glad tidings to Washington and San Francisco. At 3:00 P.M., although the wind was strong from northwest and there was an ugly sea running, she weighed anchor for home.

Beardslee thought they had completed their tests, but he was mistaken. The gale he had officially longed for had arrived. By the time the *Oregon* reached Point Conception, he had all he wanted, and more, too; but the storm did not seem to make a great deal of difference to the *Oregon*. Beardslee took advantage of the new circumstances by conducting experiments at different speeds—stopping, backing, and so forth. In a couple of hours, he had found out all he needed to know about the *Oregon*'s performance in a gale. The results were admirable.

All were overcome by weariness and wetness, and the zeal of at least some board members abated. A hasty vote was taken, all agreed that they were satisfied, and they gladly ran into Santa Cruz Harbor for the night. Early the next morning, the gale having abated, the *Oregon* started for home.

During the passage from Santa Cruz, the weather was fair, and the crewmen devoted themselves to cleaning the ship and ornamenting her with flags. A broom was set at each masthead, a symbol that signified, as in Van Tromp's day, that the ship had swept the seas of all competitors. Unknown to Scott, the men also stretched along the boats a wide strip of canvas on which was inscribed, "Scotts Got the Cramps." The message referred to the comparative record of the sister ships *Oregon*, *Massachusetts*, and *Indiana*, the first built by the Scotts, the other two by the William Cramp and Sons Shipyard, Philadelphia. It was as follows: *Indiana*, 15.6 knots; *Massachusetts*, 16.15 knots; *Oregon*, 16.79 knots. The *Oregon* was in.

As the *Oregon* entered the Golden Gate, she was met by a tug crowded with enthusiastic Californians, friends of the Scotts. The ship stopped while a few passengers came on board, caught Scott, and removed him forcibly to the tug's deck, where for a few minutes he was the most thoroughly embraced, hugged, and even kissed man in the state. San Francisco went wild again that day.

July 15, 1896, was a warm bright day in San Francisco, and the *Oregon*, officially designated as the BB-3, was ready for commissioning. Capt. Henry L. Howison, U.S.N., who had witnessed the launching of the *Oregon* three years before, had been selected as the first commanding officer of the new ship.

The ceremony that commissioned the big, turreted sea monster into service was brief but impressive. The affair was scheduled for 11:00 A.M. and its importance attracted many civilians to the ship. The officers put on their full-dress uniforms and brought their families with them. The marines and bluejackets had polished up the guns, holystoned the decks, and burnished their own accouterments and shoes. All was shipshape and Bristol fashion. The ship looked smart.

At just 11:06, Lieutenant Commander Drake, the executive officer, ordered all visitors off the aft deck, and the ceremonies began. A bugle call brought the marines, who numbered sixty, from their quarters forward. They came aft two by two with the rhythmic tread of the sea soldier and lined up in two rows along the starboard rail. A second blast on the bugle, and the bluejackets came scurrying from doors, hatches, turrets, scuttles, and even portholes—all hands from the gunner's mate to the Chinese mess boy. There were 250 sailors on board the vessel that day, and they had been divided into two watches, which lined up on either side of the big turret aft. Captain Howison and the ship's officers took their places forward on the port side.

At a nod from Howison, two sturdy bluejackets quickhauled the ensign up the flagstaff. As the flag rose skyward, its graceful folds fluttering on the morning breeze, the officers and crew uncovered in the old navy salute. The male spectators also removed their hats. Up on the main truck of the ship's mast, Captain Howison's pennant was cast loose. The long banner snapped in the wind. The captain stepped to the center of the deck and read his orders from the Navy Department, detaching him as special initiation officer of the initiation ceremonies and appointing him to command the proud new vessel. Following this, he made a speech. It was short—very short—and to the point. "This ship," he began, "has now been turned over to the navy yard and put under our charge. She has been called the guns of the navy, and is a credit to her builders. I only hope she will sustain that reputation during her commission."

Everyone applauded, the bugle sounded, the ceremony was over.

Irving M. Scott was the first to shake hands with Captain Howison after the commissioning was over.

"That was a good speech," said Scott. "Let me congratulate you." The builder and the ship's captain then walked arm in arm to the wardroom while the spectators, who numbered about fifty, ranged all over the ship. As Scott and Howison left the weather deck they could be heard talking about the most pressing military question then current: the growing possibility of a war with Spain.

# 4

# The Captain and Castile

To American naval authorities in the last decade of the nineteenth century, war with Spain seemed inevitable. Cuba was the heart of the matter. Indeed, during both the nineteenth and the twentieth centuries, that island has been a thorn in the American conscience and the source of a military threat.

During the first quarter of the nineteenth century, Americans had sympathized with the various revolutionary movements in Central and South America and seen the expulsion of Spain from her colonies in the Western Hemisphere as a natural and desired result of the impetus of their own revolution against Great Britain. The Cubans, too, had desired freedom from their European masters; yet, when invasions of Cuba were planned, first by Simon Bolivar and then, in 1825, by Mexico and Colombia, America used her influence to block the expeditions. Cuban freedom would have meant the liberation of Cuban slaves, and the United States did not want millions of free Negroes living off her coast in proximity to the slave states. As late as 1843, Daniel Webster stated that the emancipation of Negroes in Cuba would strike a death-blow to American slavery. Then commenced a series of filibustering expeditions designed to annex Cuba as a slave state. They were supported by proslavery forces in the United States. President James Buchanan even attempted to purchase Cuba, but Spain refused.

After slavery lost its political power in the 1860s, America temporarily lost interest in Cuba. But the Cubans themselves would not let American concern for Cuban affairs die. Spain had put down a Cuban revolt as early as 1826, and, during the mid-1800s, a series of Cuban and foreign attempts to liberate the island all failed. The fiasco of the Bay of Pigs had several nineteenth century antecedents. During the Grant administration, Secretary of State Hamilton Fish again broached the possibility of American purchase, but Spain turned him down.

American sympathy for the Cuban revolutionaries began to grow once again, and the *Virginius* affair cemented American antagonism towards Spain's policies in Cuba and Puerto Rico and made the war of 1898 inevitable. In 1873, the gun-running, American-registered steamer *Virginius* was overhauled on the high seas by the Spanish gunboat *Tornado* and taken to Cuba, where some fifty of her officers and crew—American citizens for the most part—were summarily shot. The American people seethed with anger and demanded war. President Grant calmly and wisely chose arbitration, and the registry of the *Virginius* proved to be false. Compensation was paid to the United States, and the incident passed; but the affair left a deep distrust for Spain in the American mind. New York–based Cuban exiles soon began to attack Spain with a sensational propaganda campaign that rivals any of the twentieth century. They were greatly aided by the yellow journalism of two influential New York newspapers, Joseph Pulitzer's *World* and William Randolph Hearst's *Journal*. Spain was portrayed as the rapist, murdering monster of the Western Hemisphere. In actuality, her antiinsurrection methods were harsh indeed, but not as barbaric as they were made out to be. In fact, they were less severe than twentieth century counterinsurgency techniques.

The guerrilla war became more vigorous as the insurgents sensed that they might defeat the weakening imperial power if they could only be patient enough—and if they could draw on American aid. Furthermore, they were beginning to develop some adequate military leaders and field commanders, such as Antonio Maceo and Mario Garcia and the accomplished guerrilla leader Gen. Maximo Gomez. In 1895, the tide of battle turned towards the rebels, and they captured most of the countryside, but Spain held the cities. The situation formed a stalemate, for the Spanish could never take back the countryside and the rebels could never capture the fortified towns. The Cleveland administration, although sympathetic to the rebels, refused to take direct action. On July 13, 1895, the Cubans won a decisive victory in the Battle of Bayamo. The Spanish Captain-General of Cuba, Martinez Campos, was forced to resign and return to Spain. He had been a humane and reasonably intelligent viceroy. He was replaced by a harsher man.

Gen. Valeriano Weyler came to Cuba on February 10, 1896, with an odious reputation for repression, cruelty, and corruption in the governance of the Philippines and in the military suppression of disorders in Barcelona. In order to destroy peasant support for the insurrection, Weyler rounded up most of Cuba's rural population and herded the people into concentration camps created for them in the garrison towns. The suffering of the peasant internees, deprived of their already meager source of livelihood, was appalling, and it touched the conscience of the rest of the civilized world. By the time the *Oregon* was

launched, Spain had one hundred fifty thousand troops
in Cuba and more on the way. In other words, a huge European army, far larger than America's regular army
(which consisted chiefly of Indian fighters), was camped
on an island only ninety miles from the coast of Florida,
and this foreign army was engaged in brutally suppress-
ing the political aspirations of the indigenous population.

When Scott and Howison chatted after the commissioning ceremony in July, 1896, they surely discussed the
strength of the Spanish fleet and the possibility of the
*Oregon*'s someday seeing action against Spanish units.

After the commissioning, Howison took the *Oregon*
on an eighteen hundred mile run to Acapulco, Mexico, to
test coal consumption at various speeds. In those days,
such a voyage was considered a long one, especially for
a battleship supposedly designed for coast defense. Upon
her return to the Golden Gate, on February 16, 1897, the
*Oregon* was ordered to Puget Sound and again battled a
severe storm without damage.

On March 20, 1897, Capt. Albert S. Barker was given
command of the ship and, in June of that year, the *Oregon* was ordered to proceed to Esquimalt, British Columbia, to represent the government at the golden jubilee
celebrating the fiftieth year of the reign of Queen Victoria.

The *Oregon* returned to Seattle on July 6, 1897, and
was placed in dry dock for overhauling. Captain Barker
and his officers proceeded to Portland, Oreg., where a
magnificent, $25,000, thirty piece silver punch set was
presented to the officers for use on the state's namesake,
the *Oregon*.

The schoolchildren of the state were given the honor
of helping to raise this sum by donating not more than
ten cents each. Adults were allowed to contribute twenty-
five cents. Contributions rolled in from all parts of the
state, and soon the order was placed in the hands of Feldenheimers Silversmiths of Portland.

Feldenheimers produced a service consisting of a
large punch bowl and dipper, a slop bowl and dipper, a

large tray, and twenty-four holders for the twenty-four crystal glasses. Each piece was beautifully engraved, the principal design being the beaver. On the side of the punch bowl was engraved the following:

FROM THE
CITIZENS OF THE STATE OF OREGON
TO THE
U.S. BATTLESHIP "OREGON"
1896

On July 6, 1897, the magnificent silver service was formally presented by Governor William Paine Lord on behalf of the people of Oregon to Captain Barker, who represented the officers and men of the *Oregon*.

Multnomah Field was chosen for the presentation, but, on account of inclement weather, the local armory was used. Because of the hurried change, a very small crowd witnessed the ceremony. The silver service was conspicuously placed on a large table, resting amid the folds of an American flag. Around the table were ranged representatives of the navy and of various state and city departments.

Mr. Dodd, chairman of the fund-raising project's committee, introduced Governor Lord, who made the presentation speech. Captain Barker accepted the service on behalf of the government and of the officers and men of the *Oregon*. After the silver service was carefully packed and ready to carry to Seattle, the floor was cleared, and an exhibition drill was performed by two hundred sailors from the monitors *Monterey* and *Monadnock*, which were anchored in Portland Harbor.

In the fall of 1897, the *Oregon* received money and authorization for the installation of rolling chocks and bilge keels, which would increase her stability in a seaway. The ship was ordered to the then-new navy yard at Bremerton, Wash., where the work was accomplished in the dry dock now designated as No. 1.

On January 17, 1898, Capt. Alexander H. McCormick,

U.S.N., took command. A month later, on February 16, a
shocking report, which had been rushed over the wires
of the transcontinental telegraph, was hurried to the office of the Bremerton Navy Yard Commandant. He read
it aloud in an incredulous tone to Captain McCormick.
The United States battleship *Maine* had been destroyed
in Havana Harbor by an explosion at 9:40 the night
before!

In December of the previous year, the United States
consul general in Havana, Gen. Fitzhugh Lee (a former
Confederate officer and a nephew of Robert E. Lee), had
become nervous about the potential threat to American
lives and property in Havana. The Cuban situation had
grown more and more ugly, and hotheaded young Spanish
officers had begun to react to the propaganda barrages
against Spain in the American press. Lee had requested
Washington to have a warship made ready to come to Havana to support him and his office if it became necessary
"to show the flag," and consequently the *Maine* had been
put on alert in Key West. She was under the command of
Capt. Charles D. Sigsbee, U.S.N., an intelligent, capable,
bespectacled officer.

An incident by a few young Spanish officers in Havana was blown up all out of proportion by the rabid American press, and President McKinley ordered the *Maine* to
sail to Havana on a "friendly" visit. At about the same
time, the Spanish cruiser *Vizcaya*, so soon to be destroyed
at Santiago, was dispatched to New York by her government "since courtesy visits had been resumed." The *Maine*
had her orders on January 24, and she sailed even though
Lee had misgivings and wished a postponement. On the
morning of January 25, the *Maine* steamed by the Morro
Castle of Havana, exchanging salutes with the fortifica-
tion, and was courteously piloted by a Spanish pilot to an
assigned mooring buoy. Sigsbee and some of his officers
went ashore on official business, but there was no liberty
for the crew, who were very unhappy indeed to be deprived
of the well-known pleasures of a Havana shore leave.

Days and nights passed uneventfully, although Sigsbee kept the *Maine* on alert even to the extent of having a steam launch patrol the ship's perimeter. Then the unforeseen took place: on the evening of February 15, there was a muffled explosion below decks followed by a tremendous blast that sent the wrecked warship to the bottom with 266 men. Only her smashed and twisted superstructure remained above the dark waters of the old harbor. Sigsbee never lost his cool, and he began an immediate investigation. Unfortunately, neither his efforts nor the work of subsequent investigations could adequately determine whether the cause of the blast was a Spanish mine or an internal explosion. A navy board suspected a mine. When in 1911 the *Maine* was finally raised and towed to sea for an honorable burial, it was still impossible to determine the cause. Modern theory is that an internal blast probably set off a magazine.

Of course, the *World* and the *Journal* tried and condemned Spain immediately and shrieked for war. Left alone in the office of Secretary of the Navy John D. Long one afternoon, the brash, young jingoistic assistant secretary, Theodore Roosevelt, sent a cable alerting Comm. George Dewey and the Asiatic Squadron to be ready to destroy the Spanish Asiatic squadron as soon as war broke out.

The *Oregon* at Bremerton was in an embarrassing position as war clouds loomed. As was the custom, she had unloaded all her ammunition at Mare Island before heading to the northern yard, so she was ordered to proceed immediately to San Francisco to get that ammo back on board.

All coal at the Bremerton Navy Yard had been used to supply ships heading for Alaska in the Klondike gold rush; so Captain McCormick could not get the *Oregon* underway until more coal reached Bremerton on March 6. Three days later, he was in San Francisco, and the crew was turning to in furious fashion around the clock, taking on ammunition, stores, and coal.

Scuttlebutt had it that the *Oregon* would proceed to Callao, Peru, from which she could conveniently depart for the Philippines or the Atlantic, as the Navy Department might decide. For once rumor proved true, and the ship was ordered to proceed on March 18 to the Peruvian port to await further orders. Only two days prior to sailing, Captain McCormick, whose health had been deteriorating, became seriously ill and had to be relieved. On March 17, the *Oregon's* third and greatest commander hastily had his steaming gear hauled aboard his new command. It was Saint Patrick's Day and, as might have been expected, Chief Boatswain's Mate "Spud" Murphy piped the new commander aboard. The heavyset, fatherly looking officer with the walrus moustache was a fifty-five-year-old veteran of the Civil War. He knew the *Oregon*, and he knew the navy. Charles Edgar Clark was his name, and he was the right man at the right time.

Clark was born in Bradford, Vt., on August 10, 1843, into an old New England family with army traditions. As a youth, Clark had hopes of entering West Point. Unfortunately or fortunately, he was unable to secure an appointment to the military academy. As something of a consolation, his kindly congressman offered him one to the United States Naval Academy, which he first declined but later accepted. Thus, on September 29, 1860, the 17-year-old lad was appointed acting midshipman.

While Clark was at Annapolis, his family moved to Montpelier, Vt., the birthplace of Admiral Dewey. Some forty years later, a local Montpelier orator would, with traditional New England humor, refer to the conflict just concluded as "the war between the village of Montpelier and the kingdom of Spain."

When Clark reported in to the academy, the school and barracks ship for fourth classmen was the United States frigate *Constitution*; so the first navy deck the young midshipman trod was the main deck of "Old Ironsides." One of Clark's favorite instructors at the academy was Alfred Thayer Mahan.

With the onset of the Civil War, the naval academy was moved from Maryland far north to Newport, R. I., for safety, and all three classes above Clark's were ordered to active service. At the academy, one of Clark's best friends and classmates was Francis A. Cook, who would command the *Brooklyn* at the Battle of Santiago and receive the surrender of the Spanish cruiser *Colon*.

During the summer of 1862, as the Civil War raged, the young midshipmen made their first practice cruise in the sloop-of-war *John Adams*. They sailed to Hampton Roads, where they saw the wreckage of the wooden-hulled *Congress* and *Cumberland*, both smashed by the *Merrimac*, and heard the details of the *Monitor*'s revolutionary success. Still, Clark was learning the trade of a windship sailor, and much of his career would be spent in wooden sailing ships—a clear example of technology being generations ahead of the imagination and practice of men.

Clark's second cruise and first trip across the Atlantic took place in the summer of 1863, as Gettysburg and Vicksburg boiled in death's cauldron. He shipped aboard the corvette *Macedonian*, commanded by the great Capt. Stephen B. Luce, U.S.N. The *Macedonian* had been captured from the British by the frigate *United States* in the War of 1812 and later rebuilt. She made for some interesting conversation in England.

In October, 1863, after only three years in the academy, Clark and his class were graduated and received their promotions to acting ensign. The young officer was assigned to the sloop-of-war *Ossipee* on station with Farragut's West Gulf Blockading Squadron. Clark joined the *Ossipe* lying off Galveston, Tex., the day before Thanksgiving.

The *Ossipee*'s patrol was the Confederate coast west of the Mississippi, and the chasing and overtaking of blockade runners constituted Clark's first combat experience. His second combat experience as a first-class raking over by Adm. David Glasgow Farragut himself, when the unfortunate ensign had to present a request for unauthorized supplies to the Flag on behalf of his own out-of-favor commanding officer. It was the only attention Farragut ever paid to young Clark, who faithfully avoided the old warrior for safety's sake from then on.

The high point of Clark's Civil War service came on the morning of August 5, 1864, when the *Ossipee* fell into line to pass the Confederate forts and attack the Southern fleet at the entrance to Mobile Bay. Clark was in charge of a division of four guns, including the forecastle pivot gun, the first of the *Ossipee*'s cannon to open fire. The ship passed the gauntlet of fire from Fort Morgan with only a few casualties and light damage, and she was equally fortunate in her passing encounter and exchange with the ram *Tennessee*. But Adm. Franklin Buchanan, senior Confederate naval officer at Mobile Bay, brought the *Tennessee* back for more. Farragut was determined to destroy the Confederacy's only capital ship, and so he ordered his squadron, one by one, to broadside, ram, and sink the damaged ironclad. The *Richmond* and the *Brooklyn* closed and poured shot and shell into the enemy vessel. Then the *Hartford* struck with her bow and was herself seriously damaged. She fired her guns furiously and at a fantastic rate.

Tied to the rigging of the *Hartford*, Farragut waved the *Ossipee* on. The *Ossipee*'s throttle was wide open, and the wooden ship raced to a collision with the ironclad. On the forecastle, Clark suddenly saw a Confederate officer appear above the casement of the *Tennessee*, waving a white flag. Clark raced aft to the captain to report and then transmitted to the *Tennessee* the captain's order: "Put your helm to starboard! Ours is to port." But it was too late, and anyway the wheel ropes of the *Tennessee* had been shot away. The *Ossipee*, her engines backing full, nevertheless struck hard, but neither ship sank. The *Tennessee*, the last hope of the Confederate navy in the gulf, then surrendered to the *Ossipee*.

After the war, Clark began thirty-three years of peacetime duty as a naval officer serving a nation that had little interest in sea power or military affairs but preferred to expend its energies in the westward movement, in binding up the nation's wounds, and in prodigious economic expansion. His career was typical, his advancement unspectacular within the shackles of a most rigid seniority system.

Clark's first duty after the war was in the U.S.S. *Vanderbilt*, a side-wheeler donated by Commodore Vanderbilt to the United States government during the Civil War. Clark had two promotions on the *Vanderbilt*, to the grade of master on May 10, 1866, and to lieutenant on February 21, 1867. His next ship was the U.S.S. *Sewanee*, a double ender. Aboard the *Sewanee*, he passed the examination for promotion to lieutenant commander and reached that grade on March 12, 1868, at the age of twenty-four. It would be thirteen years until his next promotion.

At six o'clock on the morning of July 7, 1868, the *Sewanee* was cruising off the northern end of Vancouver Island with Clark the officer of the deck. Running at full speed with a following current of almost three knots, she struck an uncharted rock and was instantly ground into a total wreck. All the crew made it ashore, and Clark soon found himself in charge of a party of shipwrecked sailors on Hope Island waiting for rescue and holding off hostile Indians. Clark's group was eventually rescued by the Royal Navy.

Clark was detached from the Pacific Fleet and ordered home. On his way to Montpelier, he stopped off at Greenfield, Mass., to renew his acquaintance with the family of his classmate George T. Davis and particularly with Davis's youngest sister, Louisa. They were married on April 8, 1869: a naval officer generally has little time to waste. They would have two daughters, both of whom married officers in the United States Navy.

In July, 1870, Clark was assigned as navigator of the monitor *Dictator* with the Atlantic fleet. Two months later, he left the *Dictator* and began his first shore duty,

as an instructor and assistant to the commandant of midshipmen at the naval academy, where he stayed until 1873.
After the academy tour, Clark was assigned as executive
officer on another monitor, the U.S.S. *Mahopac*. Ordered
to the Asiatic Squadron in February, 1874, Clark and his
family rode the trains across country to San Francisco
and then sailed on the S.S. *Colorado* to Yokohama. There
Clark reported to Rear Adm. Alexander Mosley Pennock,
who was flying his flag on Farragut's beloved *Hartford*.
Pennock assigned Clark to the U.S.S. *Yantic* as executive
officer. She was lying off Shanghai, and Clark had to leave
his family at Nagasaki.

After seven months on the *Yantic*, Clark was ordered
to the *Hartford* as executive officer and later wound up
as executive officer of the U.S.S. *Monocaci*, a light draft
paddle-wheeler. The *Monocaci* was one of the first of the
Yankee gunboats on the China Station, and Clark finished his Asiatic tour in the Yangtze upwater.

In August, 1881, after two years of shore duty at the
Boston Navy Yard, Clark reported to the U.S.S. *New
Hampshire*, an old ship-of-the-line that was fitting out
for the training of naval apprentices. The old sailing ships
were the boot camps of the day. On November 15, Clark
was promoted to commander and given control of the *New
Hampshire*, usually a captain's billet.

Clark's next duty afloat was the command of the
U.S.S. *Ranger*, a bark-rigged, screw propeller steamer
fitted out for survey work in the North Pacific. Among
his subordinate officers involved in the hydrographic work
was Ensign Albert A. Ackerman, U.S.N., who would command one of the *Oregon*'s turrets at the Battle of Santiago.
The work on the *Ranger* was grueling, and, when his cruise
was completed, Clark welcomed five years of shore duty,
mostly as a lighthouse inspector on the Great Lakes.

In May, 1894, Clark was given command of the steam
sloop-of-war *Mohican* and placed at the head of the Bering Sea Patrol, a squadron of ten vessels, with orders to
enforce the sealing regulations recently agreed upon by

arbitration in Paris. Clark's service in this capacity was outstanding. On June 21, 1896, he was promoted to captain. Other duty on the Pacific coast followed, including command of the receiving ship *Independence* and of the monitor *Monterey*, from which he was detached on March 15, 1898, with emergency orders to leave San Diego as soon as possible and proceed to San Francisco to take immediate command of the battleship *Oregon*.

*Oregon,* 1898 (U.S. Bureau of Ships)

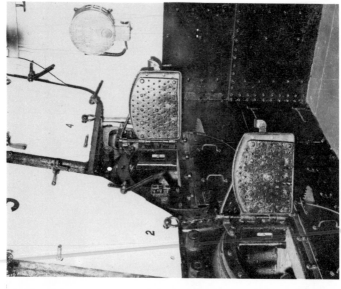

*Oregon* Fireroom (Oregon Historical Society)

*Oregon* 13-inch gun breech (Oregon Historical Society)

Moving the *Oregon* to Marine Park at the foot of S. W. Jefferson Street, Portland, September 11, 1938 (Oregon Historical Society)

Removing the mast for the Battleship *Oregon* Park, 1942 (Oregon Historical Society)

*Oregon*, 1898 (U.S. Bureau of Ships)

Captain Charles E. Clark in his cabin, April, 1898 (Oregon Historical Society)

President and Mrs. Wilson boarding to review the Pacific Fleet, August 21, 1919 (Navy Department)

Captain Charles E. Clark with Naval Cadet Overstreet and the captain's orderlies: Marine Corps
privates Haight (rear left) and Ellis, on the
bridge of the *Oregon* during battle with the
Spanish Fleet, July 3, 1898 (Oregon Historical
Society)

*Oregon* at the Union Iron Works, San Francisco, preparing for
sea trials, March 8, 1896 (San Francisco Maritime Museum)

Dress Ship, 1918 (Navy Department)

Hull of *Oregon*, Guam, 1948 (Oregon Historical Society)

# 5

# "Six Thousand Miles to the Indian Isles"

Clark had only forty-eight hours on board the *Oregon* before she had to shove off for the long and dangerous run to the east coast to join the American Battle Fleet. (The crew, for security reasons, did not know whether they were heading for Cuba or the Philippines.) Forty-eight hours to take on the last of 1,600 tons of coal, 500 tons of ammunition, and enough stores for six months. The ship stepped deep into the water. All hands toiled around the clock. Clark himself was exhausted when, early on the morning of March 19, 1898, the *Oregon*—displacing almost 12,000 tons and short twenty-seven men in the black gang and sixty-seven hands on deck—departed her birthplace and began a voyage that would live in history.

The officers of the *Oregon* on this voyage are listed in Appendix B. William D. Leahy, an engineer cadet on the cruise, became one of the nation's great military leaders of World War II.

Orders were to make for Callao, Peru, four thousand miles away, as fast as possible. The *Oregon* would average 250 nautical miles per day, an excellent cruising clip for a ship supposedly designed as a coast defense battleship. The one problem that arose as she moved towards the equator was that of ventilation in the firerooms and other engineering spaces, where temperatures rose to the range of 110 to 150 degrees.

As soon as the *Oregon* cleared San Francisco Bay and all divisions reported secure for sea, Clark commenced such battle drills as clearing ship for action, gunnery drill, and damage control. The drills would continue all through the voyage and, indeed, up to the very day of battle in July. As with Isaac Hull and Thomas Truxtun, drill was Clark's text and sermon of military service. The only day off in the sixteen-day run to Peru was when the *Oregon* crossed the line. King Neptune was piped aboard to receive his customary honors due.

However, Clark did allow the ship's band to present a concert each evening on the boat deck before tattoo. It played the popular dance tunes of the Gay Nineties. Also, Clark would gather his officers in the wardroom for a game of whist. From the beginning, Clark evidenced that superb but rare mixture of humaneness and strength that forms the core of the kind of leadership that evokes devotion.

A week out of San Francisco, Chief Engineer Milligan informed Clark that, with the boilers continuing to make a full head of steam, the supply of fresh water for the crew would have to be severely limited. The engineer rightly did not wish to impair the efficiency of his boilers by contaminating them with salt water. Clark was deeply concerned for the health and endurance of his crew, for not only would drinking water be limited, but it would be available only in the form of hot, distilled feed water. He called all hands, except those on watch, topside to explain.

In his autobiography, *My Fifty Years in the Navy*, Clark would write:

When I explained to the men, however, that salt water in the boilers meant scale, and that scale would reduce our speed, delay us in getting to the seat of war, and might impair our efficiency in battle, the deprivation was borne without a murmur. The very small quantity of ice that was made on board went to the firemen and coal passers, and however much the rest of us may have longed for a little to cool the lukewarm drinking water, I know that it was not only willingly, but cheerfully given up.[1]

Milligan had another idea: Why not save for an emergency the best coal on board, the "dusky diamonds" from Cardiff, Wales, taken on board in San Francisco? The quality of coal was an extremely important factor in a warship's ability to operate to her maximum capability. Purer coal meant hotter fires, more steam, and thus more speed. It also meant less ash to be hauled topside and "deep sixed." Clark agreed, and, underway and at night, the willing crew redistributed the coal in the bunkers so that Cardiff coal was in a standby position. Coaling ship—that most filthy, backbreaking, and despised job—was miserable even in port with unlimited water available for washing; but handling vast amounts of the black fuel at sea, aboard a rolling ship and without fresh water to wash with, was even more miserable. After the job was finished, decks, equipment, and men were all flushed down with salt water dipped from the sea.

On arriving at Callao, Clark was disappointed to hear that the board of inquiry appointed to look into the circumstances that led to the sinking of the *Maine* had not yet announced its findings. He was informed by the Navy Department that the Spanish torpedo boat *Temerario* had been reported off the east coast of South America but that its destination was unknown. When this intelligence reached the crew, the word was passed that, if the *Oregon* were ordered to the Atlantic and the *Temerario* were met in the Strait of Magellan, Captain Clark intended to sink the Spanish ship, war or no war.

The Peruvians seemed to strongly favor the United

States in her threatened war with Spain. But it was also reported that some of the Spanish residents of Callao and Lima were plotting to sink or blow up the *Oregon*. Rumor or fact, Clark took no chances and ordered the sentries doubled. During the hours of darkness, a steam launch patrolled around the ship to detect and investigate approaching boats, and its searchlights were kept at the ready.

On April 6, Clark received word that the board of inquiry had blamed Spain for the *Maine* disaster. With this news came word that the Navy Department had definitely decided to use the *Oregon* and the *Marietta* in the Atlantic. The bunkers of the battleship were immediately filled with 1,100 tons of coal that Commander Symonds, captain of the U.S. gunboat *Marietta*, had purchased for the *Oregon* before her arrival in Callao.

The *Oregon* set sail on the morning of April 7, 1898, after fifty hot, backbreaking, tense hours in Callao. Clark knew that Spanish intelligence had made inquiries as to the day and time of the ship's intended departure, and so she slipped out quietly, aided by a fog bank, with only Clark aware of her destination. She would try to slip past the Spanish Atlantic squadron, commanded by Adm. Pascual Cervera y Topete, and join the American fleet assembling off the Florida coast. This fleet would soon be under the command of William T. Sampson, who would be promoted from captain to rear admiral and ordered by President McKinley to blockade Cuba. While the *Oregon* was still en route to Florida, diplomatic relations between the United States and Spain would break down, efforts at international mediation would fail, last-minute Spanish concessions to Cuba would prove unacceptable to an enraged American public, and Congress would declare on April 25 that a state of war existed between the United States and Spain as of April 21.

Heading south, the *Oregon* forced 12 to 13.5 knots and handled beautifully, even when shipping heavy seas from the steadily worsening weather along the coast of

Patagonia. Despite the storms, the gun crews were exercised each day with subcaliber firing and small arms practice. On April 16, the *Oregon* was running before a moderate gale, visibility extremely limited, and trying to make the entrance to the Strait of Magellan. Finally, the weather broke for a moment, and Clark could see the Evangelistas and Cape Pillar. He ordered full speed to try to make the safe anchorage at Tamar Island while there was still some light left, but the storm increased to a full gale, and the ship could not make the anchorage before nightfall. Clark was worried. He knew the shores were littered with the wrecks of a hundred ships, sail and steamer. He ordered soundings from the chains, but to no avail. The seas prevented accurate readings. Clark decided to try to anchor and ordered one let go. With a wild rush and a shattering roar, the anchor cable flew out 125 fathoms before the smoking brakes could check it. At last, it bit into the ground, and the other anchor was paid out under foot. The anchors held, and the *Oregon* was safe, but not a sailor undressed or slept a wink that night.

At first light the next morning, the anchors were weighed, and the *Oregon* was soon racing through the narrowest reaches of the strait, chased by a heavy snow storm, with sheer black cliffs looming to port and starboard. Towards evening, the crew sighted Cape Froward, the extreme tip of the continent, and at night the ship came to anchor at Sandy Point. The passage of 165 miles had been made in eleven hours with the fireroom blowers increasing the natural draft of the funnels. A remarkable speed for a battleship of the day.

Now the crew expected to meet the Spanish torpedo boat *Temerario*, and all guns were loaded and manned, while constant lookout was maintained "below and aloft." Coaling proceeded at Sandy Point or Punta Arenas. The fuel was purchased from a Scottish agent and had to be taken from a hulk in which wool had been stored on top. The crew worked hard, and the agent made things more difficult by insisting that the hoisting buckets be frequently weighed. As one bucket reached the *Oregon*'s weather deck, Chief Murphy, in Irish exasperation at Scottish tightness, yelled down to the agent: "Here! Lower again for another weigh! There's a fly on the edge of that bucket!"

The gunboat *Marietta*, mounting six guns, joined the *Oregon* at Sandy Point. She coaled too and participated in the security patrol by launches.

At first light on April 21, the two vessels sailed in consort under sealed orders. That afternoon, the *Oregon* spoke to an American steamer en route from Montevideo to the Klondike. The steamer signaled that there were "prospects of peace." It was the day on which hostilities would officially be considered to have begun.

The ships, however, sailed on a strictly war footing: no lights carried, guns loaded, searchlights ready, the crew sleeping at their battle stations. Clark was taking no chances. The *Marietta*, a slower ship than the *Oregon*, was nevertheless ordered to scout ahead. The *Marietta* tossed barrels in her wake, and Clark had his gun crews at target practice whenever possible, using small arms inserted in the barrels of the big guns so as to test aim and accuracy without wasting precious large-caliber ammunition.

The gunboat could only make ten knots in calm seas, and the South Atlantic slowed her to eight. Nearing Rio de Janeiro, their next port of call, Clark ordered the *Marietta* to proceed independently and sent the *Oregon* racing ahead. The *Oregon* made Rio on the afternoon of April 30, with the rail manned, "The Star-Spangled Banner" and "Hail Columbia" blaring from the ship's band, and cheers broadsiding the Brazilian fleet and waterfront. The battlecry was "Remember the Maine!"

There the *Oregon* learned that war had been declared. Another ship was waiting to join Clark's armada, and a supply of coal was ready. The additional consort was the dynamite cruiser *Nictheroy*, purchased from the Bra-

zilians for $1 million (to buy friendship as well as a war-
ship) and later renamed the *Buffalo*.

It was back to the coal barges for the crew. The dispatches from the Naval War Board in Washington, on
which Alfred Thayer Mahan was sitting, again said, "Beware the *Temerario*." The enemy vessel supposedly had
left Montevideo and was headed for Rio. The *Oregon* would
never see the *Temerario*.

Clark moved the *Oregon* to an unusual anchorage in
mid-harbor, where no vessel would have an excuse to ap-
proach. He informed the Brazilian admiral that Brazil
was expected to prevent any hostile acts by Spanish vessels in neutral waters, and that the *Oregon* would sink
any Spanish vessel that approached within half a mile of
her anchorage.

The Brazilian government proved friendly and readily agreed to the demands. The American steam cutters
patrolled all night, the searchlights were in use, and the
rapid-fire guns were always manned. The *Marietta* anchored as picket vessel in a position to cover the entrance
to the harbor. At night, the Brazilian admiral sent a
cruiser to patrol outside the harbor entrance, and with
her searchlights and those from the forts, it would have
been impossible for a Spanish ship to enter the harbor
unseen. Sentries were placed on the coal barges, for Spanish sympathizers with bombs in their possession had
been apprehended near them, and all coal was carefully
examined before it was put on board.

On May 2 came the news of Dewey's superb victory
in Manila Bay. The great commodore, with a small squadron of cruisers led by the *Olympia*, had crushed the Spanish Asiatic squadron in a single morning and won an empire for his country. Only one American life had been
lost. Clark himself heaved a deep sigh of relief: his son-
in-law was serving with Dewey.

The scene that followed the publication of this news
in Rio might be likened to an Indian war dance, for the

coal-blackened men fairly went wild. They danced on the coal barges and decks. The entire American colony, including the American minister, came on board to celebrate.

Meanwhile, the officers were carefully and secretly considering the dispatch from the Navy Department: "Four Spanish armored cruisers, heavy and fast, three torpedo-boat destroyers sailed April 29 from Cape de Verde to the west. Destination unknown. Beware of and study carefully the situation. Must be left to your discretion entirely to avoid this fleet and to reach the United States by West Indies. You can go when and where you desire. *Nictheroy* and *Marietta* subject to the orders of yourself." [2]

Captain Clark's answer to the department was as follows: "The receipt of telegram of May 3 is acknowledged. Will proceed in obedience to orders I have received. Keeping near the Brazilian coast, as the Navy Department considers the Spanish fleet from Cape de Verde superior, will be unsuitable. I can coal from the *Nictheroy*, if necessity compels it, to reach the United States. If the *Nictheroy* delays too much I shall hasten passage leaving her with the *Marietta*. Every department of the *Oregon* in fine condition." [3]

A last exchange of dispatches with the Naval War Board in Washington led to some confusion as to orders, and Clark's final dispatch read, "Don't hamper me with instructions. I am not afraid, with this ship, of the whole Spanish fleet."

Mahan and other members of the Naval War Board were deeply concerned about the lack of security in Washington and the refusal of American newspapers to keep the movements of naval vessels a secret. Therefore, the board decided that the best way to ensure the *Oregon*'s safety was to leave Clark at loose ends and allow him to make his way to Florida as best he could without requiring him to clear his itinerary with Washington. The *Oregon* was a vital and exposed portion of the American naval force.

Thus, at seven o'clock on the morning of May 4, the *Oregon* and the *Marietta* steamed majestically out of Rio's harbor. Many of the good people of Rio believed the ships were going to certain destruction, for the city's newspapers had printed startling rumors that Admiral Cervera's fleet awaited the Americans outside the harbor. The Brazilian admiral even sent a cruiser out ahead of the *Oregon* and the *Marietta* to prevent an engagement in his nation's territorial waters.

At the request of the government of Brazil, the *Oregon* and the *Marietta* had agreed to sail twelve hours before the *Buffalo* did. The vessels went about fifty miles and then returned to meet the *Buffalo*. Both ships lay off the harbor entrance all night and left before daylight to prevent detection; but the *Buffalo* did not come out, and so Clark sent the *Marietta* back towards Rio to wait another twelve hours. After Clark had waited thirty-six hours in all, he sighted the *Buffalo* coming out with the *Marietta*; but as the *Buffalo* could not make more than seven knots, the question arose whether the *Oregon* and the *Marietta* should remain with this slow vessel or continue northward at high speed. The *Oregon* would be an important addition to Admiral Sampson's fleet; the department had been urging Clark to make a quick passage; the enemy's fleet was supposed to be seeking the *Oregon*, and Clark felt that she could make a better fight single-handed than if accompanied by slow vessels that would have to be protected. The captain weighed all these considerations and decided to part company with the two other vessels and proceed north at full speed. So, in the middle of the night, Clark signaled the *Marietta*, "Proceed with the *Buffalo* to Bahia, and cable the department." The *Marietta* answered, "Good-by and good luck." Then the *Oregon* went ahead full speed.

The following day, upon the high seas, Clark summoned all hands aft to the quarterdeck and read the men part of a message from the Navy Department stating that the Spanish fleet was supposed to be in search of the

*Oregon.* A scene of great enthusiasm followed: five hundred men joined in an outburst of cheers for the *Oregon,* her captain, and her officers. Every preparation was made to meet the enemy's fleet. The ship was cleared for action. All the woodwork was torn out. Even the expensive mahogany pilothouse was reduced to a skeleton to prevent its being set on fire by Spanish shell. The ship was painted the dull gray war color, and the graceful white vessel that had steamed out of Rio harbor was transformed into an ugly lead-colored fighter. To lessen the danger of conflagration, preparations were made to throw all boats overboard upon sighting the enemy's fleet. Everybody was eager for action at any odds.

Before leaving Rio, the *Oregon's* men had purchased a large supply of red ribbon and used it to make cap bands. Letters cut from brass and attached to the bands spelled out the inspiring words, "Remember the Maine." The cap of every *Oregon* man bore this legend throughout the war.

The battleship steamed northward along the coast of Brazil, intending to touch at Bahia or Pernambuco to communicate with the Navy Department. One forenoon was spent at target practice. All the guns were fired and the shooting was excellent.

On May 8, after dark, the *Oregon* anchored in the harbor of Bahia, and early next morning Clark sent the following cable message to Washington: "Much delayed by the *Marietta* and the *Nictheroy.* Left them near Cape Frio, with orders to come home or beach, if necessity compels it, to avoid capture. The *Oregon* could steam fourteen knots for hours, and in a running fight might beat off and even cripple the Spanish fleet. With present amount of coal on board will be in good fighting trim, and could reach West Indies. If more should be taken here I could reach Key West; but, in that case, belt-armor, cellulose belt, and protective deck would be below water-line. Whereabouts of Spanish fleet requested."[4] Clark made arrangements for coal, but in the evening this answer to the captain's message was received: "Proceed at once to West Indies without further stop Brazil. No authentic news the Spanish fleet. Avoid if possible. We believe that you will defeat it if met."[5]

And so, in the middle of the night, the ship went to sea, standing well off the coast in order to make a wide sweep around Cape St. Roque, where Admiral Cervera's fleet was rumored to be lurking. Captain Clark's plan of battle was as follows: Upon sighting the Spanish fleet, the *Oregon* would sound general quarters, go ahead full speed under forced draft, and head away from the enemy. The purpose of this maneuver was to "string out" the enemy's vessels in their chase. When their leading vessel came within close range, the *Oregon* would turn on her and attack her with heavy broadsides. Clark hoped to destroy the first enemy vessel and then devote attention to the others in succession. He was confident that not more than two of these vessels could equal the *Oregon*'s speed; by making a running fight, he expected to eliminate the possibility of the enemy's surrounding and either ramming or torpedoing the American vessel.

About eight o'clock on the evening of May 12, off Cape St. Roque, the *Oregon* sighted a number of lights, which had the appearance of a fleet sailing in double column. Not a light was burning on the *Oregon*, and she passed right through the midst of the vessels undetected, for she could not have been seen a hundred yards away. What those lights were has never been ascertained, but, according to the log of the *Colon*, one of Cervera's fleet, the enemy's squadron was not off Cape St. Roque at that time.

Of course, the *Oregon* passed many sailing vessels. They included the tiny sloop *Spray*, in which one of history's greatest mariners, Capt. Joshua Slocum of New Bedford, Mass., was making the first solo voyage around the world. Slocum described the passing:

> On the 14th of May, just north of the equator, and near the longitude of the river Amazon, I saw first a mast, with the Stars and Stripes floating from it,

rising astern as if poked up out of the sea, and then
rapidly appearing on the horizon, like a citadel, the
*Oregon*! As she came near I saw that the great ship
was flying the signals "C B T," which read, "Are
there any men-of-war about?" Right under these flags,
and larger than the *Spray's* mainsail, so it appeared,
was the yellowest Spanish flag I ever saw. It gave me
a nightmare some time after when I reflected on it
in my dreams.

I did not make out the *Oregon's* signals till she
passed ahead, where I could read them better, for she
was two miles away, and I had no binoculars. When I
had read her flags I hoisted the signal "No," for I
had not seen any Spanish men-of-war; I had not been
looking for any. My signal, "Let us keep together for
mutual protection," Captain Clark did not seem to
regard as necessary. Perhaps my small flags were not
made out; anyhow, the *Oregon* steamed on with a rush,
looking for Spanish men-of-war, as I learned after-
ward. The *Oregon's* great flag was dipped beautifully
three times to the *Spray's* lowered flag as she passed
on.[6]

Meanwhile, in the inferno of the battleship's firerooms, the carbon filament electric light bulbs glowed red
in a haze of coal dust, with which the ventilators, wind
funnels, and port hold scoops were unable to cope. Grimy
stokers, stripped to the waist and streaming with sweat,
threw shovelsful of coal on the fires, slammed the fur-
nace doors, and winced with pain as the muscles in their
backs protested their efforts to straighten up.

On May 15, the *Oregon* made 375 miles, her longest
one-day run of the voyage. At daylight on May 18, she
came to anchor in the harbor of Bridgetown, Barbados.

The first news that greeted Clark was that the American navy had bombarded San Juan, Puerto Rico, and had
been repelled. Actually, the attack, under Admiral Sampson's command, had been of an exploratory nature. Bridgetown placed the *Oregon* in quarantine because she had
been in two yellow fever ports—even though no one had
been allowed on shore in those ports and all on board were

in good health. The white inhabitants of Barbados were strongly pro-American, and boatloads of them pulled around the ship, cheering and wishing her success. The blacks shouted, "American bully boys! You knock Spanyard in a cock hat, and then we give you a good time."

Her Majesty's officials were most friendly and gave Clark a cordial welcome, but they rigidly enforced the neutrality laws. The *Oregon* was allowed sufficient coal to reach a home port, but she could remain in Bridgetown only twenty-four hours. Neither of the belligerents was supposed to receive cable messages until twenty-four hours after the ship's departure. Before the government censor reached the cable office, the American consul had managed to send a dispatch to the State Department announcing the *Oregon*'s arrival. Therefore, the Spanish consul was permitted to cable news of the *Oregon*'s arrival to his government. In Bridgetown, Clark heard a rumor that a Spanish fleet of sixteen vessels was at Martinique, only ninety miles away, and that Spanish vessels had been seen cruising off Barbados the previous day. He seemed to have the enemy's vessels all around him.

The *Oregon* began coaling as soon as possible, and, to the anxious inquiries of a few shore people—most likely Spanish informers—Clark stated that he should probably sail next morning. But about nine o'clock that night, the *Oregon* suddenly cast off the coal barges and steamed out of the harbor. She kept all lights burning brightly and set a course direct for Key West, so that the Spanish spies could see the lights and report to the Martinique fleet the direction in which the *Oregon* had sailed. But when she was five miles from the harbor, she suddenly extinguished every light, turned about, made a sweep around Barbados, and laid a course well to the east of all the islands. This strategic move was designed to frustrate any night attack by the enemy torpedo boats and armored vessels that were believed to be at Martinique. The *Oregon* passed north of the Bahamas and after dark on May

24, anchored off Jupiter Inlet, Fla. From there she sent the Navy Department the following dispatch: "*Oregon* arrived. Have coal enough to reach Dry Tortugas or Hampton Roads. Boat landed through surf awaits orders." The announcement of her safe arrival soon sent a thrill of joy and thanksgiving throughout the United States.

About two that morning came this answer: "If ship is in good condition and ready for service, go to Key West, otherwise to Hampton Roads. The department congratulates you upon your safe arrival, which has been announced to the President." The anchor was hove up in a hurry, and, with light and happy hearts, the crewmen were soon on their way to Key West, planning to eventually join Admiral Sampson's fleet in Cuban waters. The *Oregon* reached Key West on the morning of May 26 and anchored off Sand Key. She had made the run of 14,500 miles in just sixty-six days; passed through two oceans and circumnavigated a continent; endured most oppressive heat and incessant toil; demonstrated to the skeptics of Europe that heavy battleships of the *Oregon* class could cruise with safety under all conditions of wind and sea; and, at the end of this voyage, had the pleasure to report the ship in excellent condition and ready to meet the enemy.

Clark, who had so ably executed his trying task, received congratulatory messages from every part of the United States, including this telegram from Secretary of the Navy Long: "The department congratulates you, your officers and crew, upon the completion of your long and remarkably successful voyage."

All hands were called to muster on the evening of May 26, and Captain Clark read the congratulatory telegram from the Secretary of the Navy. Almost immediately, the U.S.S. *Wilmington* crossed the bows of the battleship and gave her the first "Three cheers for the *Oregon*."

The distances made on this long voyage are taken from the official log of the *Oregon*:

San Francisco to Callao, Peru .... 4,112.0 nautical miles
Callao, Peru, to Port Tamor
  (western end of
  Strait of Magellan) .......... 2,549.0 nautical miles
Port Tamor to Punta Arenas
  (eastern end of
  Strait of Magellan) ........... 131.4 nautical miles
Punta Arenas to
  Rio de Janeiro, Brazil ......... 2,247.7 nautical miles
Rio de Janeiro to Bahia, Brazil ... 741.7 nautical miles
Bahia to Barbados,
  British West Indies .......... 2,228.0 nautical miles
Barbados to Jupiter Inlet, Fla. ... 1,665.0 nautical miles

Forty-one hundred tons of coal were used during the voyage, and the average speed was 11.6 knots per hour. The *Oregon* traveled a total distance of 14,500 miles from Bremerton, Wash., to Jupiter Inlet, Fla.

The *Oregon*'s nautical achievement had many repercussions in naval circles. It was now realized that battleships could swiftly steam to any part of the world. If a battleship was well built and properly kept up, it could be ready for immediate service upon arrival and need not be dry-docked for extensive repairs. Battleships could be coaled in port or from rendezvousing colliers upon the high seas. The ship's performance hinged on the quality of its machinery; its engineers' skill in preventing machinery breakdowns from poor maintenance or ill usage; and the structural integrity of the hull. The *Oregon* excelled in all these factors.

Naval theoreticians like Mahan, however, began to wonder if the voyage around the tip of South America should have taken place at all. If American ships of the Pacific Fleet were to be called to action in the North Atlantic, they should not have to sail fourteen thousand miles to do so. The race of the *Oregon* and its strategic implications were not lost on military thinkers. Nor would Theodore Roosevelt (who had recently resigned as Assistant Secretary of the Navy and, as a lieutenant colonel of volunteers, was raising a regiment of cavalry) forget the voyage of the *Oregon*. The lesson of her race—against the storms of the South Atlantic, the Spanish enemy, and time itself—would be one of the major arguments 'for the building of the Panama Canal. The navy would have to be able to proceed rapidly between the Atlantic and the Pacific.

# 6

# Into Battle

The nation had greeted Dewey's Manila Bay victory of May 1, 1898, with joyful abandon. For the first time since the Civil War, Americans had a great naval hero to celebrate. But along the east coast, the jubilation quickly turned into a fearful hysteria. The Spanish fleet (commanded by Adm. Pascual Cervera y Topete, a dignified, white-haired, experienced naval officer) was on the high seas headed west, destination unknown. At any moment it might appear off an American city and shell the community to rubble. "Where is the navy?" every coastal village from Maine to Florida inquired. Congressmen began to pressure the navy to distribute units of the fleet along the seaboard to protect the cities. But such a policy would have been disastrous.

Alfred Thayer Mahan had shown the American nation the importance of a united fleet, or a "fleet-in-being."

Scattered units would be unable to stop an attack by a concerted enemy naval force, for fleets could only defeat other fleets in mass action. Fortunately, the navy had not forgotten the lessons of the War of 1812. United States vessels won many individual actions in that war, but the American navy was ultimately defeated because its units were foolishly assigned to the protection of ports. The Royal Navy bottled up American ships in the ports, and as a result won local superiority anywhere it wished to be. The coastal settlements and even the capital of the United States became playthings for British landing parties. In 1898, the Atlantic Fleet was divided into squadrons, but it would finally assemble when Cervera was located and would fight and win as a battle unit.

At the beginning of the Spanish-American War, neither the American navy nor the Spanish navy had overwhelming superiority on paper. The United States had four fast, armored cruisers; Spain had seven. Spain's torpedo boats were considered among the best in the world, and torpedo boats in general were thought of as most deadly and even decisive weapons. However, the Spanish were unable to get their one battleship out of dry dock in time for service in the war. In addition, their state of readiness, their logistical support, and their leadership would prove far below the standards of the United States Navy.

Since February 15, when the *Maine* was destroyed, the U.S. naval force in southern waters had been stationed on war footing at Key West and the Dry Tortugas. The men were already well trained in gun mechanisms and manuals, for such training was usual in time of peace. To this training was added constant daily target practice with subcaliber fire. The practice consisted of firing a small projectile from a large gun, employing the pointing and aiming mechanisms of the latter. A small gun was placed inside the breech of the large gun, precisely in its center, and was held there by a special fitting. The axes of the small and large pieces therefore coincided and, except for the shock and recoil, normal firing conditions with full charge were imitated. One-pounders were ordinarily placed inside the heavy turret guns, and rifle barrels were used with the secondary batteries.

During those waiting days at Tortugas and Key West, fluttering flags a few hundred yards from each ship showed the targets, and for hours each day the splash of bullets followed the rifle reports with monotonous regularity. After each shot, the gun was swung off the target, brought back, and aimed anew, thus making each shot an independent exercise. It was not inspiring or dramatic, this steady burning of powder in small quantities during the sultry afternoons; but it was the sort of work that makes war deadly, and it bore its fruit in the swift and terrible destruction of Cervera's fleet.

The Navy Department had directed that all vessels should be painted a uniform gray, the "war color," to diminish as much as possible their visibility under the varying conditions of the atmosphere. The complement of each vessel was increased to its war-time number, and the commander in chief, Rear Adm. William F. Sampson, U.S.N., awaited his instructions. A number of additions to the squadron had arrived, for the government had already begun to purchase and equip auxiliaries.

In addition to Sampson's force, which was known as the North Atlantic Squadron, a second force called the Flying Squadron had been organized at Hampton Roads and placed in command of Com. Winfield S. Schley, U.S.N. The Flying Squadron was intended as a compact force for expeditionary work. The cruiser *Brooklyn* was the flagship of this squadron, which also included the battleships *Massachusetts* and *Texas* and the fast cruisers *Columbia* and *Minneapolis*. Later, a third squadron, known as the Northern Patrol Squadron, was formed under the command of Com. J. A. Howell, who was recalled from the Mediterranean. His principal vessels were the flagship *San Francisco*, the ram *Katahdin*, and a few steamers that had been purchased from the Morgan Line and converted to armed auxiliaries. The Northern Patrol

Squadron was to protect the northern Atlantic coast from Spanish raids. But neither the Flying Squadron nor the Northern Patrol Squadron actually saw service until they were sent to Cuban waters after the appearance of Cervera in the West Indies. At that time, they ceased to exist as independent commands and were placed under the orders of Admiral Sampson.

The double-turreted monitors were fitted out as speedily as possible and sent to Key West. The old single-turreted monitors, which had long been lying in the back channel at Philadelphia's League Island and were useless except as floating batteries, were placed in the northern ports. There, manned by naval militia and aided by armed tugs and other improvised auxiliaries, they formed an inner line of naval defense and a psychological placebo for nervous coastal dwellers.

The war began for the Atlantic Fleet of the United States Navy on April 26, 1898, when Sampson's squadron of eleven ships and four torpedo boats weighed anchor and departed Key West to blockade Havana. By May 1, it was known that Cervera's squadron of four armored cruisers and two torpedo boats had sailed from Cape Verde, presumably for the West Indies. Cervera's first port of call was likely to be far to the east of Cuba at San Juan, Puerto Rico, a Spanish fortified port with a good harbor and ample supplies of coal. The San Juan expedition was organized in the hope of finding Cervera's fleet in San Juan or of meeting it in that vicinity. The expedition consisted of the flagship *New York*, the battleships *Iowa* and *Indiana*, the monitors *Amphitrite* and *Terror*, the cruisers *Detroit* and *Montgomery*, the torpedo boat *Porter*, the armed tug *Wompatuck*, and the collier *Niagara*. The vessels rendezvoused north of Bahia de Cadiz light, near Cardenas, and sailed at midnight on May 4. But Cervera was not at San Juan. Lacking a naval foe, Sampson bombarded the city on May 12. It was an indecisive, perhaps even an unnecessary, action.

The squadron steamed slowly back to Key West, the

slow and unwieldy monitors being taken in tow. Instructions were sent to the auxiliary cruisers employed as scouts, and the naval base at Key West was cabled to have coal ready for all the ships.

By this time, Admiral Cervera had reached the Caribbean. His four cruisers were heavily armed and armored ships, rated at a trial speed of twenty knots and presumably capable of making sixteen knots under service conditions. His torpedo boats were new, very fast, the best product of English yards. They were twice as large as their American counterparts, the *Dupont* and the *Porter,* and were also more seaworthy. For their class, they were heavily armed. The destination of this squadron was unknown to the Americans. Cervera was probably heading for Cienfuegos or Havana, but he might have been planning to reach Santiago de Cuba or San Juan.

Cervera's purpose, if he knew his business, would be to raid the blockade and break it at various points, but especially at Havana; to avoid action with U.S. battleships; to destroy cruisers and auxiliaries; and perhaps, if he could maintain his coal supply, to make a dash at points upon the northern coast. It was difficult to estimate the damage such a squadron might do, with good luck and bold and skillful handling. Therefore, it was vitally important to find Cervera's fleet and either destroy it or shut it up in a closely blockaded port. The search for Cervera became the paramount object of the war.

On May 17, Sampson's flagship *New York,* which was heading for Key West, put on a full head of steam and left the remainder of the squadron to follow. At six that evening, she met the torpedo boat *Dupont,* which carried important dispatches confirming the impression that Cervera would attempt to get into either Cienfuegos or Havana. Arriving at Key West at 4 P.M., May 18, Sampson found Schley's vessels coaling. The *Iowa* arrived at dark, and the other ships of the San Juan expedition early the next morning. All the vessels coaled as quickly as possible. The light vessels on the blockade had been warned against surprise, and the *Cincinnati* and the *Vesuvius* were scouting the Yucatan Channel.

Plans were at once made for new dispositions. Commodore Schley, with the cruiser *Brooklyn*, the *Massachusetts*, the *Texas*, and the *Scorpion*, sailed on the morning of May 19 for Cienfuegos by way of Cape San Antonio, the western end of Cuba. The next day, the *Iowa*, the gunboat *Castine*, the collier *Merrimac*, and the torpedo boat *Dupont* were dispacthed to Cienfuegos to join him, and, on May 21, the cruiser *Marblehead*, the yacht *Eagle*, and the auxiliary gunboat *Vixen* were sent on the same business. The resulting U.S. force on the southern side of Cuba was strong enough to destroy Cervera or to blockade him in Cienfuegos. Cervera was known to have left Curaçao on May 15. If his destination were either Santiago or Cienfuegos, he had already arrived. He had in fact entered Santiago at about the hour of Schley's sailing from Key West.

When the *Oregon* reached Key West on May 26, Sampson's hand was strengthened. On May 27, the ship's crew was increased by the arrival of sixty young men of the Chicago naval reserves. They remained with the *Oregon* until she went to New York after the war, and they won the respect and esteem of the battleship's regular officers and men. Several years after the war, they formed an organization named the Clark Club, which royally entertained Captain Clark on two occasions when he visited Chicago.

At Key West or later off Santiago, the crew was augmented by Lt. C. M. Stone, Ens. L. A. Bostwick, and Naval Cadets P. B. Dungan, E. J. Sadler, C. C. Kalbfus, H. J. Brinser, C. G. Hatch, C. Schackford, and T. C. Dunlap. All served through the war. A. G. Magill, a naval cadet who sailed on the *Oregon* from San Francisco, had become seriously ill on the run from the Pacific and been sent home.

The *Oregon* was coaled and supplied, and she weighed anchor once more at 1:04 A.M. on May 29. She had had

less than three days in port after a 14,500-mile cruise.
Her engines were fully functioning, her boilers reasonably clean, and her crew healthy and in high spirits. She
had not needed an overhaul. The *Oregon* was indeed a superb ship, probably the finest ship the United States had
built to that time.

Clark was under orders to join the blockading squadron off Havana led by Com. John Crittenden Watson,
U.S.N., who had been Farragut's flag lieutenant on the
*Hartford* during the Civil War. The *Oregon* arrived off
Havana on May 29, a bright Sunday morning. She was
greeted with enthusiasm by the ships of Watson's squadron, and her crew was cheered wildly as she passed down
the line of warships to the blare of the bands of the blockading ships. Still tired and dirty from coaling ship, Clark's
men beamed with satisfaction at their reception: once the
elusive Spanish fleet had been located and brought to bay,
they'd show the other ships of the United States Navy
what the *Oregon* could really do.

They did not have long to wait! Soon after daybreak
the next morning, May 29, Commodore Schley's Flying
Squadron, after much unnecessary delay, steamed in toward the Morro at the entrance to the harbor of Santiago
on the southern coast of Cuba and discovered three ships
lying at anchor near Smith Key. One of them had a military mast between her two smokestacks and was immediately identified as the *Cristobal Colon*, one of Admiral
Cervera's biggest ships. The Spanish fleet was in the harbor of Santiago de Cuba!

The *St. Paul*, a former liner that had been acting as
a scout for Schley's squadron, was immediately dispatched
to St. Nicholas Mole, Haiti, where the nearest cable office
was located, to telegraph the news to Washington and to
Admiral Sampson in Key West. Sampson received the
message at lunchtime and immediately ordered the flagship *New York* and the converted yacht *Mayflower* to
prepare to get underway. The two ships sailed from Key
West on May 30, contacted Commodore Watson's squad-

ron off Havana that afternoon and, after ordering the
*Oregon* to accompany them, steamed around the eastern
tip of Cuba and joined Commodore Schley at Santiago at
six on the morning of June 1.

Soon after the arrival of the three ships off the steaming tropical coast, Commodore Schley went aboard the
*New York* to make his report to Admiral Sampson. While
the two officers were conferring, Captain Clark signaled
the *Brooklyn*, the flagship of Schley's squadron, requesting orders. He was told to "proceed six miles to the south-
ward and report names of strange vessels." The order
was actually an assignment to a station in the southern
part of the blockading line, but Clark took the wording
literally and set out in the direction indicated. The *Oregon*
soon spotted smoke on the horizon ahead. In a moment,
the battleship was off in full pursuit, with her boilers under forced draft. As she gained speed and closed in on her
"prize," a lookout incorrectly reported that the stranger
was a large steamer and that cargo was being jettisoned.
A few minutes later, the "enemy ship" was close enough
for the officer of the deck to identify her as a large tug.
When a blank charge was fired across her bow, the tug-
boat came about and hoisted the Stars and Stripes. She
was a newspaper boat with a number of correspondents
aboard, bound for Jamaica with dispatches for their pa-
pers. A battleship chasing a tug! The crestfallen *Oregon*
turned back toward the blockading line and, at the half-
way mark, met the cruiser *Marblehead*, which had been
sent in pursuit as soon as the flagship had discovered the
*Oregon*'s mistake. Although steaming at fifteen knots,
the fast cruiser had been unable to overtake the battleship, and, as the two ships passed, the *Marblehead*'s men
sent up a cheer for the battleship they couldn't catch.

The Navy Department was unwilling to expose Sampson's fleet to the fire of the Santiago shore batteries,
which the ships would have to pass in order to engage the
Spanish warships. For this reason, the admiral continued

Commodore Schley's blockade. The American ships arranged themselves in a semicircle facing the mouth of the bay. If the Spaniards appeared, the Americans were to converge on the bay's outlet and engage the enemy's ships as they came out. Admiral Sampson decided to try to "put a cork in the bottle" at Santiago, even though he had witnessed the futility of a similar maneuver at Charleston, S.C., during the Civil War. At Charleston, the federal commander had tried to obstruct the entrance to the bay by scuttling in the channel a number of old New Bedford whalers loaded with stones. Sampson proposed to prevent the escape of the Spanish fleet by sinking the collier *Merrimac* in the fairway at Santiago.

From the hundreds who volunteered for the risky mission, a crew of seven was finally selected, and Lt. Richmond P. Hobson of the Naval Construction Corps was placed in command. The seven took the old collier into the narrow passage at 4:00 A.M. on June 3. The ship was detected by the Spanish batteries, which opened fire and damaged the *Merrimac*'s steering gear so badly that she overshot her mark, failed to turn athwart the channel, and sank too far inside to block the entrance. The volunteers took to the boats and were rescued by Cervera himself, who gallantly reported their safety to Sampson next morning. Hobson would receive the Congressional Medal of Honor for his great courage.

The tedious, month-long blockade was underway, with no end in sight. The ships were cauldrons of steam and sweat. The men wore as few clothes as they could get away with; the officers wore unpressed, pajama-like dress whites, made limp and shapeless by the moisture. Engineroom or boilerroom duty was hell. Most of the captains shut down boilers to relieve the black gang and save coal, but Clark wisely kept all fires lighted throughout the blockade. When the Spanish finally made their break for freedom, only the *Oregon* was able to get up full steam during the course of the battle.

Clark suggested to Sampson that the semicircle of American ships off the harbor entrance did not constitute a tight enough ring and that picket boats should be employed close in. Sampson agreed, and the *Oregon*, the *Massachusetts*, and the *New York* provided the boats and crews. Sampson also wisely decided to use the ships' large searchlights to illuminate the harbor entrance at night. This time the *Oregon*, the *Massachusetts*, and the *Iowa* got the duty. The *Oregon* in her turn steamed well within enemy rifle range and turned her light to the harbor. It was dangerous duty, but Cervera would later say that the light prevented him from trying a nighttime escape.

Meanwhile, the United States Army was gathering at Tampa. The regular army had been called in from the West, and volunteer units poured in. They included the Rough Riders—the First United States Volunteer Cavalry under Col. Leonard Wood and Lt. Col. Theodore Roosevelt.

There were not enough supplies to keep the men in Tampa and not enough transports to take them anywhere else. After the government finally decided that Sampson should not brave the batteries and mines at Santiago's harbor, the army was ordered to attempt an amphibious operation near the city to take the forts and guns by land. Each army unit had to scramble for a place on the limited number of transports (chartered merchant vessels for the most part), and the Rough Riders found themselves embarked on June 8 sans horses and most of their equipment. The rest of the army fared no better.

To make things worse, the loaded convoy did not get underway until June 14 due to a false report of a Spanish raiding squadron in the vicinity. The poor soldiers had a week of hell, crammed abroad overloaded ships in the Florida sun.

On June 10, before the Army could shove off, the first American troops landed in Cuba. They were the United States Marines. The United States had only one more requirement to assure the successful maintenance of the blockade, and that was to possess a safe harbor near Santiago for shelter, coaling, and repairs. Admiral Sampson secured this indispensable adjunct by sending the *Marblehead* and the *Yankee* to Guantanamo. On board the former was the *Oregon*'s marine guard under the command of Capt. Randolph Dickens, U.S.M.C., and Lt. A. R. Davis, U.S.M.C. Sampson's ships drove the Spanish gunboats to the inner harbor and secured the outer harbor, which was excellently suited to the needs of the fleet. To make possession both useful and complete, it became necessary to gain a position on shore and drive back the enemy so that the Spanish could not annoy the ships and boats in the bay. This work was assigned to the *Marblehead* and *Oregon* marine guards and to the First Marine Battalion, which left Key West on June 7 and arrived in Guantanamo Bay on June 10 aboard the transport *Panther*.

The marine guards spearheaded the amphibious assault under cover provided by the *Marblehead*'s guns. They splashed ashore closely followed by the First Marine Battalion in boats from the *Panther*, supported by shore bombardment from the *Yankee*. The marines established themselves on a low hill where a Spanish blockhouse had been destroyed by the guns of the *Yankee*. The next evening, they were attacked by Spaniards concealed in the chaparral, and two men on outposts were killed. The attack was renewed in the night by the unseen enemy, and Surgeon Gibbs was killed and two privates wounded. The next day, the camp was shifted to a better position, and some sixty Cubans joined the Americans. The Spanish bombarded the camp all that night, and Sergeant Good was killed, but on the thirteenth, with the aid of the Cubans, who knew the country, the Spanish were easily repelled. On the fourteenth the Americans took the offensive. Two companies of marines, supported by the Cubans, left the camp at nine o'clock that morning to destroy the well at Cuzco, which was the Spaniards' only water supply within twelve miles. They failed to cut off the enemy as they had hoped, but they drove the Spaniards steadily before them, reaching the intervening hill first and carrying the crest under a sharp fire. As the marines descended into the valley, the Spaniards broke cover and retreated rapidly, and at three that afternoon the fight was over, the well filled with earth, and the heliograph signal station captured and destroyed. One Spanish lieutenant and seventeen men were captured, and the prisoners reported a Spanish loss of two officers and fifty-eight men killed and a large number wounded. On the American side, one marine was wounded and about a dozen were overcome by heat. This engagement marked the end of the Spanish attacks at Guantanamo. The Spaniards had had enough and withdrew, leaving the American post undisturbed to the end of the campaign. The marines had done their work admirably. For three days and nights, they had met and repelled the attacks of a concealed enemy. Then they had taken the offensive, and they had marched and fought for hours under the tropical sun and through dense brush with the steadiness and marksmanship of experienced bushfighters.

The guard from the *Oregon* seemed destined to see stormy service, for, after the Spanish-American War, at least half the guard was assigned to the legation guard at Peking. In the siege of the Chinese capital during the Boxer Rebellion, many of these men were killed and hardly one escaped unwounded. Lieutenant Davis was killed at Tientsin.

The army finally arrived off Santiago at daybreak of June 20, and Sampson immediately met with the army commander, Gen. William R. Shafter, U.S.A., as well as with the Cuban generals Garcia and Castillo. The point of the operation was to take the forts around Santiago and thus capture the Spanish ships by land or flush them out into the range of the waiting American guns offshore. Shafter, however, refused to land his men just beyond the Morro as Sampson demanded. Instead, the force landed some ten miles down the coast at Daiquiri and had to drive through the jungle against a courageous Spanish rearguard action. The Americans were struck down by bullets, heat, and fever, and they gained less than a mile a day.

But first the troops had to be landed. The army had neither lighters nor launches. They had been omitted, forgotten, or lost, and no one knew exactly how or where; so the work of disembarking the troops fell to the navy. The ships provided a cover of a heavy fire, and the landing was effected without any resistance from the enemy. On an open coast, without any harbor or shelter, with nothing but an iron pier so high as to be useless, smoothly, rapidly, efficiently, through a heavy surf, on the beach and at an unfloored wooden wharf, the boats and launches of the navy landed fifteen thousand soldiers with a loss of only two men. It was a neat piece of work, thoroughly and punctually performed, and it excited admiration among foreign observers, who had recently beheld with disbelief the comic performances connected with the embarkation at Tampa.

The next morning Gen. Joseph Wheeler, commanding a division of dismounted cavalry under direct orders from General Shafter, rode forward, followed by two squadrons of the First Volunteer Cavalry and one each of the First and Tenth Regular Cavalry. The campaign had begun.

To lighten the monotony of blockade duty and to soften up the defenses of the bay, Sampson decided to stage a full-dress bombardment of the forts at the harbor entrance. On June 26, he formed his fleet into parallel lines some eight hundred yards apart and steamed the ships toward the island until a scant two miles of water separated them from their objective. Breakfast was served, and, at 8:00 A.M., the flagship *New York*, leading the eastern line which was directed at the Morro fort, sent an eight-inch shell curving toward the ancient stronghold. Commodore Schley's flagship *Brooklyn*, which was leading the western line, followed suit in less than a minute with a shot aimed at Socapa Point. As the firing became general, the two lines of ships began maneuvering with faultless precision, Sampson's squadron turning toward the east and Schley's toward the west.

The lighter ships stayed out of range of the shore batteries, but the battleships steamed slowly in toward the land, firing as they advanced, until the range had been reduced to eighteen hundred yards. The replies from the forts, weak at first, became hotter as the gunners evidently gained confidence. But the Spaniards' marksmanship was poor, and none of the American ships received material damage while scoring again and again on the coquina and masonry walls of the fortifications.

An eyewitness described the scene:

> It was hard for the untrained eye looking under the smoke from the cannon's discharge, to follow the course of the shell; but there was no mistake as to where it landed. When the shells hit soft spots on the cliffs and exploded, they sent reddish earth and stones hurtling skyward. Others struck point-blank and burst into radiating fragments, which left thin lines of bluish smoke trailing after them. Sometimes a shell plunged into a huge crevice and exploded out of sight, but in a moment huge boulders that had been loosened would tumble downward into the sea. At one point the cliff was like flint, and shells rebounded and hurled off without producing any effect. Occasionally these deflections were in straight lines, and again a vicious, corkscrew whirling gave a vivid idea of the fearful force of the projectile. The terrific impact made the shells glow with heat as they spun upwards into the clouds, or bounded straight back as if seeking to return to the ships from which they had been fired.

The cannonading was continued for $2\frac{1}{2}$ hours before Admiral Sampson signaled the fleet to retire. During the engagement, the military mast of the *Oregon* was struck by a piece of shell, and the mast of the *Massachusetts* received a direct hit without suffering serious damage. One seaman injured by a bursting shell was the only casualty in the fleet. The Morro fort was badly hit by the bombardment. Some of the shells landed uncomfortably close to the cells in which the men of the *Merrimac* were confined, but none was hurt.

A mood of quiet satisfaction reigned aboard the *Oregon* that evening as her crew went about the task of cleaning up after the morning's work. After the final engagement at 6:30 P.M., Seaman R. Cross found a secluded spot in the shelter of the after thirteen-inch turret, drew a stub of pencil from the pocket of his jumper, and settled himself to make an entry in his diary:

> June 26. Started in this morning to see if we coulden knock down that Spanish old Morro or else knock something cruckit around it. Well we pelted away for an hour or more and the flag ship signalled over to the Iowa to close in and pump at the Smith Key Battry. The Iowa signalled back that her forward Turret was out of order, so it fel to us, we went in to 700 yards of the shore Battry and did knock down the Spanish flag with an 8-inch shell and knocked over one of the three Big Guns. I believe if the flag ship had not called us off Capt. Clark would have went in along side of old Morro and give him a tutching up.

Two days later Seaman Cross made another entry:

> June 28. I am getting tired to trying to keep cases on this thing. There is nothing doing but laying around here like a lot of sharks watching for a fish.[1]

For the Army the taking of the blockhouse on San Juan Hill (actually Kettle Hill) on July 1, 1898, by the Rough Riders under Roosevelt (now a full colonel and commanding officer of the regiment) was the most distinguished action of the brief and confused but successful campaign. During the battle on July 1, the *Oregon* joined the other ships of the combined squadrons in supporting the army by bombarding the city of Santiago. At 5:00 A.M. on July 2, she took part in a second bombardment of the batteries on both sides of the entrance to the harbor. This bombardment succeeded in silencing the batteries along the shore line. The shelling completely destroyed the Punta Gorda battery behind the Morro and further damaged the fort.

Sunday morning, July 3, 1898, dawned clear and bright off the harbor of Santiago. The red ball of the sun rose swiftly in the eastern sky, and the day promised to be fiercely hot and breathless. The glossy surface of the blue sea reflected the gray hulls of the warships swinging lazily at anchor. At 8:45 A.M., Admiral Sampson's flagship, *New York*, made signal, "Disregard movements of commander in chief," and headed eastward with the *Hist* and the *Ericsson*. Sampson was on his way to a conference with General Shafter at Siboney, a few miles down the coast. The *Massachusetts* was coaling at Guantanamo.

The United States fleet was formed in a semicircle three miles off the harbor. With the departure of the *New York*, the semicircle tightened and drew in. Lined up from east to west were the auxiliary gunboat *Gloucester*; the battleships *Indiana*, *Oregon*, *Iowa*, and *Texas*; the cruiser *Brooklyn;* and the auxiliary gunboat *Vixen*. Commodore Schley on the *Brooklyn* was senior officer present afloat and nominally in charge, although for the most part the ensuing battle was a captain's fight.

The men on the American vessels were carrying out the Sunday morning routine that had been followed since the squadrons had arrived on station. Breakfast had been eaten, and the final morning tasks of cleaning ship before mustering at quarters were nearing completion. A press boat passed the *Oregon*, and a reporter shouted the news that the army had suffered heavy losses in the previous day's attack on the city.

Three bells in the forenoon watch were about to be struck as the clock in the pilot house of each ship stood at 9:28. The bugle sound of "quarters" had just been carried away on the breeze. Clad in spotless white uniforms, the men of the fleet mustered in divisions on their ships to listen to the monthly ritual of the reading of the Articles of War, which would normally be followed by church call and divine services. On the *Oregon*, Clark was in his cabin buckling on his dress sword and putting on his cap to go on deck when suddenly the brass gongs of the ship's alarm rang furiously and Clark's orderly burst into the compartment shouting: "The Spanish Fleet, sir! It's coming out!"

The *Oregon*'s sharp-eyed chief quartermaster had spotted the masthead of a ship slipping out from behind Smith Cay. "Battle Stations!" The signal "enemy is escaping" was rushed aloft, and a six-pounder gun fired as a warning to the other vessels. After thirty-four days of waiting and watching, the moment of battle had arrived. The *Oregon* bluejackets rushed to their guns and stations with almost childlike eagerness and anticipation as well as a sense of relief that the long watch was at last over. They threw themselves down scuttles and ladders, desperate to get to battle stations at the boilers, engines, hoists, and guns.

Clark rushed on deck. Men shouted to him as they pointed shoreward: "There they come! There they come! You'll see them in a minute, Captain. She's behind the Morro now!" The armored cruiser *Infanta Maria Teresa* appeared, Cervera's blue flag and her great red and yellow battle ensigns standing out sharply against the green jungle behind her. It was forced draft and full speed for the *Oregon*, the only American ship ready for emergency speed.

The orders poured from the conning tower now:
"Turn on the current for the electric hoists!"
"Steam and pressure on the turrets!"
"Hoist the battle flags!"
"Lay aloft range finders in the top!"
"Range to the lead ship!"
"Set sights for 4,000 yards!"

Commodore Schley signaled: "Clear ship for action" and "Close up."

Down the shore, Sampson heard the first cannon firing and ordered the *New York* to turn about and steam for the sound of the guns. As Cervera's flagship cleared the Morro, she turned westward, and the *Oregon* opened up with her eight-inch guns. The armored cruiser *Vizcaya*, the second-class battleship *Cristobal Colon*, and the armored cruiser *Oquendo* followed the *Maria Teresa* in a column, each opening fire as her guns would bear. The American vessels nearly collided with each other in their eagerness to close with the enemy. The *Brooklyn*, at the western end of the line, suddenly found the entire Spanish squadron pointing for her midships, and she was forced to turn away to starboard, narrowly missing the American battleships as she turned 360 degrees to reengage the enemy outboard of the equally speedy *Oregon*, the leading American battlewagon.

As the *Oregon* passed Santiago Harbor, the Spanish torpedo boat destroyers *Pluton* and *Furor* made a most ill-timed appearance and received a full volley from the *Oregon*'s six-inch guns and rapid-fires. The other battleships hit too. The small ships were crushed by a hail of projectiles. The *Furor* disappeared as a lump of twisted iron beneath the waves, taking Adm. Fernando Villaamil down with her. The *Gloucester*—under Comdr. Richard Wainwright, U.S.N., former executive officer of the *Maine* at Havana—closed with the *Pluton* and drove her ashore. The Spanish torpedo boat destroyers had lasted twelve minutes in battle. The *Oregon* was all speed. An officer of the *Iowa* would later describe her thus:

> The *Oregon* came racing across the *Iowa*'s bow and charged right down on the Spanish fleet, letting go first at one vessel, then at the other, and all the time carrying a great white bone in her teeth, that told of her engine-power and wonderful speed.

Clark ordered the *Oregon*'s head a point more westward. "Head them off, and let the land trap them," thought Clark, almost like an old Indian fighter. To his surprise, the *Oregon* was not only passing through the pack of the American battleships that had started the engagement west of his ship, but she was also overtaking the supposedly speedier Spanish cruisers! He could not know how much damage the Spanish vessels had suffered in breaking out of the harbor. In fact, the American shells had not hulled them but had smashed their wooden decks and superstructure. Horrible fires were beginning to make torches of the fleeing vessels, their speed fanning the infernos. Also, the Spaniards' main propulsion machinery was in poor repair, and the hulls were foul.

Seeing all but the *Brooklyn* falling back, Clark grinned and said to his navigator, "Well, Nicholson, it seems we shall have them on our hands after all." The men of the *Brooklyn*, the most lightly armed vessel of the American squadron, saw the *Oregon* coming on strong and fast and shouted, "Here comes the *Oregon*! It's the *Oregon*, God bless her!"

Schley's flagship was skippered by Clark's old Annapolis roommate, Capt. F. A. Cook, U.S.N. At Schley's order, he signaled, "Follow the flag." It wasn't necessary.

Suddenly the *Teresa* seemed to slow, and the other Spanish ships steamed past her. Was she mortally wounded or was the gallant Cervera sacrificing himself and the flagship to make a stand and perhaps save the other three ships of his squadron? At 10:00 A.M., the Spanish flagship was the prime target of the *Oregon* and the pursuing battlewagons. At two thousand yards, the forward guns of the *Oregon*, with the *Teresa* sharp on her starboard bow, poured everything into the wounded vessel. By 10:10, the *Teresa* was a roaring hellfire, her guns silenced, smoke and flame leaping from her upper works. The stricken ship turned and limped to the beach and grounded at Juan Gonzales, only six miles from the harbor of Santiago. She had seen only forty minutes of actual combat. The *Brooklyn* and the *Oregon* leaped on for further prey. The *Iowa* and the *Texas* followed, and the *Indiana* trailed far behind. Last of all was the *New York*, puffing up coast as fast as she could to get a piece of the action Sampson had so long awaited and planned for. Passing the *Indiana,* Sampson ordered that ship to turn back to the harbor to watch for the *Reina Mercedes,* which had remained in port.

With the *Teresa* a burning wreck, the *Oregon* turned her attention to the *Almirante Oquendo* and began firing on the cruiser with her forward guns and all those in her starboard broadside that could be brought to bear. Closing to a range of nine hundred yards, the American battleship subjected her victim to "the hottest and most destructive fire of the eventful day." Within twelve minutes, the *Oquendo* was ablaze and headed inshore. The *Oregon* drew up abeam of the Spanish ship and raked her unmercifully. The *Oquendo* continued to fire until her torn and battered hull came to rest on the beach only a half mile west of the *Teresa.* Captain Clark shouted over the noise of the guns, "We have settled another; look out for the rest." The *Oregon's* gunners answered him with a cheer that was repeated down through the ammunition passages and the magazines to the steaming boilerroom and engineroom below.

Lt. R. F. Nicholson suggested that they turn about and completely destroy the *Oquendo.* Clark answered, "No, that's a dead cock in the pit. The others can attend to her. We'll push on for the two ahead." And so the bones of the *Oquendo* were left for the slower ships astern to pick over.

It was all bulldog determination now on the *Oregon.* The Americans had the Spanish on the hip and could end the war in a day.

The *Vizcaya* was next in line and two miles away when the *Oregon* turned her forward thirteen-inch guns on the fleeing cruiser. The *Brooklyn,* which had been on the battleship's port bow since the chase began, had been firing on the *Vizcaya* for some time and was taking hot fire from the Spanish ship. When the signal "close up" broke on the flagship's signal halyards, the *Oregon* repeated the message to the ships astern and increased her speed to sixteen knots. The range had dropped to 3,000 yards when the *Vizcaya* swung offshore and headed across the *Oregon*'s bow while continuing to fire her forward guns at the *Brooklyn* and those on her port side at the *Oregon*. This maneuver brought the *Vizcaya* broadside to the battleship, but after a thirteen-inch shell from the *Oregon* struck the port bow of the Spanish ship, she turned back on her original course. A few minutes later, another thirteen-inch shell struck the *Vizcaya* amidships, causing her to heel to starboard while a column of steam and smoke erupted from her superstructure. To the accompaniment of cheer after cheer from the men of the *Oregon*, the *Vizcaya* headed for shore with flames bursting from her hull.

While the *Vizcaya* was under fire from the *Oregon* and the *Brooklyn*, Captain Clark had been moving about the deck of his ship commending his gunners for their accuracy and warning the men not to expose themselves unnecessarily. At the moment the Spanish ship turned toward the beach, Clark was talking to the after turret's gunnery officer, who was deploring the fact that he could not bring his guns to bear while the quarry was so far ahead. When Clark saw the Spanish cruiser change course, he cried, "There's your chance! There's your chance!" and the six-inch guns of the *Oregon*'s starboard broadside and the thirteen-inch guns of the after turret blasted the *Vizcaya*'s upper works. By the time the *Oregon* had the cruiser to starboard, the *Vizcaya* had had enough. Her colors came down on the double, and she ran ashore at Aserraderos, eighteen miles from the Morro—the third burning wreck in ninety minutes. Commodore Schley promptly acknowledged the battleship's support with the signal "*Oregon*, well done."

Clark stood on the top of the forward thirteen-inch turret, his favorite conning position during the chase. He felt no great sense of jubilation or victory. He was a sensitive, compassionate, and fatherly man. Later, he would reminisce about the *Vizcaya*:

As this last battle-torn wreck of what had once been
a proud and splendid ship fled to the shore like some
sick and wounded thing, seeking a place to die, I could
feel none of that exultation that is supposed to come
with victory. If I had seen my own decks covered with
blood, and my officers and men dying around me,
perhaps resentment would have supplied the necessary
ingredient, but as it was, the faces of the women and
children in far-away Spain, the widows and orphans
of this July third, rose before me so vividly that I had
to draw comfort from the thought that a decisive
victory is after all more merciful than a prolonged
struggle, and that every life lost to-day in breaking
down the bridge to Spain might mean a hundred saved
hereafter.[2]

The unfortunate *Vizcaya* had caused the only American casualty of the action. A shell from one of her guns struck Chief Yeoman George Ellis, U.S.N., of the *Brooklyn* and killed him instantly. He had been taking ranges with the stadimeter for the forward turret and had stepped out to try to see beyond the smoke of battle. The shell passed over the *Brooklyn* herself.

Suddenly, for the *Oregon* and the *Brooklyn*, the great chase began. The *Cristobal Colon* was escaping. She was Spain's newest and fastest vessel. The *Oregon* poured on the coal and was soon making over sixteen knots. The *Brooklyn*, sheering off somewhat to port in order to intercept the enemy at a distant headland, signaled, "She seems built in Italy." Clark retorted, "She may have been built in Italy but she will end on the coast of Cuba." He was not wrong.

The *Cristobal Colon* was six miles ahead of the *Oregon*, but the American vessel was overtaking. The Spanish ship was running out of her good coal, and her second-rate fuel was inadequate to keep up the necessary steam pressure. Also, the Spanish crewmen were exhausted because they had been serving as infantry against the American army until the day before. The Spaniards had been stiffened up by large rations of alcohol, which now was taking its toll.

Clark sent his men to dinner by watches; but, after getting a bite, they returned on deck to follow the exciting chase and take a pull at their pipes. As the *Oregon* dashed onward, slowly gaining and soon to be within range, the enthusiasm reached high pitch. Old Boatswain's Mate Murphy, stationed in the fighting-top, gave way to his excited feelings and yelled through a megaphone, "Oh, captain, I say, can't you give her a thirteen-inch shell, fer Gawd's sake!" The men in the engineer force, ever unmindful of the frightful heat, were straining every muscle to its utmost, and the engineering officers were helping the exhausted firemen feed the roaring furnaces.

Several times, the *Colon* turned in as if looking for a good place to run ashore; but, each time she changed her mind and continued to run for her life. It was 12:50 when Captain Clark gave Lt. (jg) E. W. Eberle orders to "try a thirteen-inch shell on her," and soon a 1,100-pound projectile was flying after the *Colon*. The chief engineer was just coming on deck to ask the captain to fire a gun in order to encourage the exhausted engineer force; when the men below heard the old thirteen-incher roar, they knew they were within range and made the effort of their lives.

The scene on the *Oregon*'s decks was one of unbridled enthusiasm. The chase was nearly over. Officers and men were crowded on top of the forward turrets, and some were aloft—all eager to see the final work of that historic day. The *Brooklyn* fired a few eight-inch shells, and the *Oregon* fired two of the missiles; but all fell short, and the eight-inch guns ceased firing. The *Colon* returned a few shots, but they fell far short of their mark. *Oregon*'s forward thirteen-inch guns continued to fire slowly and deliberately, with increasing trajectory. The sixth shot, at a range of ninety-five hundred yards (nearly five miles), dropped just ahead of the *Colon*, which then suddenly turned and headed for the shore. The men were cheering wildly. A few minutes later, at 1:12, a thirteen-

inch shell struck under the _Colon's stern_. It was a near
miss, close aboard. Immediately, the _Colon_'s colors dropped
in a heap at the foot of her flagstaff. Her bugle sounded,
"Cease firing!" The Spanish ship had surrendered, and
the last shot of July 3 had been fired.

Suddenly, the thunder of heavy guns was replaced
by the strains of "The Star-Spangled Banner" from the
_Oregon_'s band. On the forward deck, 550 men—mostly
bare to the waist, and begrimed with powder, smoke, and
coal dust—were embracing one another and cheering
with the fervor and joy that mark the outpouring of the
hearts of men who have looked into the face of death and
known unequivocal victory. There were rousing cheers
for Captain Clark; cheers from the _Brooklyn_, which signaled, "Congratulations upon the glorious victory"; and
a wildly enthusiastic return in kind from the _Oregon_.

After lowering her colors, the _Colon_ ran ashore at Rio
Tarquino, one of the most beautiful spots on the south
coast of Cuba, about fifty miles west of Santiago and
thirty-two miles beyond the _Vizcaya_'s resting place. The
_Colon_'s demoralized crew fell to destroying her armament
and equipment.

At the time of the _Colon_'s surrender, the _Brooklyn_
was off the _Oregon_'s port bow. Between six and seven
miles astern and hull down were the _New York_ and the
_Texas._ These two vessels and the _Vixen_ joined the _Ore-
gon_ at about 2:20, just as the _Brooklyn_'s boat was returning from the _Colon_. All commanding officers were
ordered to report on board the _New York_. As Captain
Clark's gig approached the flagship, he received an ova-
tion from the crew of the _New York_. Clark rose in his
boat, tipped his hat, and ordered his boat crew to rise and
receive the cheers of their fellow sailors.

Clark soon returned from the flagship with orders
to head east with the _Brooklyn_ and blast the Spanish battleship that was reported off Siboney. But just as they
were ready to start, the _New York_ learned that the reported Spanish battleship was an Austrian vessel. The

flagship signaled, "*Oregon*, take charge of prize and haul her off the beach."

It was after 4:00 P.M. When the prize crew reached the *Colon*, they found fifteen feet of water in her engine-rooms and all valves open. The prisoners were immediately sent aft on the quarterdeck and were soon transferred with their effects to the *Resolute*.

Five cows were found tied up on the *Colon*'s forecastle, and some of them succeeded in swimming ashore after the *Oregon*'s men had cut them adrift. Souvenirs taken included several battle flags, pictures of the ship and officers, a captain's gig, two cutters, a dog, two cats, some chickens, and a black pig. The *Colon*'s pig became the *Oregon*'s mascot and was promptly named Dennis Blanco: *Dennis* because all his predecessors in the navy had borne that name, and *Blanco*—well, probably because he was of the opposite color, so very black.

Officers and men worked furiously to keep the *Colon* afloat; but their efforts were in vain, for, at 11:00 P.M., she listed to starboard and turned over on her side. The *Oregon*'s officers left just as she went over. The American flag had been hoisted and went down with her. The *Texas* and the *Oregon* remained by the wreck all night, and the next morning they started for their station at Santiago. The *Oregon* slowly steamed up the bend past a scene of horror that silenced all hands. The burning and battered wrecks strewn along the beach made too pitiful a picture for rejoicing. Floating about were uniforms, boxes, trunks, planks, and the bloated bodies of the Spanish dead.

When the *Oregon* reached Santiago, Commodore Schley greeted her with the signal "welcome back, brave *Oregon*." It was July 4, and although the officers and men of the squadron didn't know it then, they had won the war on a summer morning.

Engineer in Chief George W. Melville, U.S.N., Chief of the Bureau of Steam Engineering, discussed the *Oregon*'s achievement in his annual report of 1898:

It has not been customary to call special attention to the performance of vessels except on trials under maximum conditions, but that of the *Oregon* is so exceptional that it deserves a record in the Bureau's report. She was ordered from the Pacific to the Gulf before war was declared, and leaving Puget Sound 6 March, arrived at Jupiter Inlet 24 May, having steamed over 14,500 miles, stopping only for coal, and not being delayed an hour anywhere through any derangements of the machinery. Stopping at Key West only long enough to coal, she took her place in the blockading fleet at Santiago, and was always ready for service.

This alone would have given her an unparalleled record among battleships but the culmination came in the great battle of 3 July, when she surpassed herself. Always ready for action, she speedily attained a power greater than that developed on the trial, giving a speed (on account of greater displacement and foul bottom) only slightly less than then attained, and distancing all the other ships except the *Brooklyn*, which is 5 knots faster. Every official report comments on her wonderful speed, and it is generally believed that but for it, one at least, and possibly two, of the Spanish ships might have escaped.

The whole record is thus one which has never been equaled in the history of navies, and it will remain the standard for a long time to come. The credit is due, in the first place, to the builders—the Union Iron Works—for the excellence of the material and workmanship, but still more, and chiefly, to the engineering department of the vessel. The Bureau, therefore, takes great pleasure in commending to the Department's most favorable consideration Chief Engineer Robert W. Milligan, the executive head of the department, for his professional ability, untiring care, and excellent discipline, and also the junior engineer officers and the enlisted men, whose faithfulness and zeal, and under most trying circumstances, have enabled our Navy to add this to the other brilliant records of our vessels.[3]

# 7

# Mopping Up

On July 4, 1898, the victorious American ships were back on station off Santiago. The blockade had to be maintained because the army was closing in on the city and Spanish transports might attempt an evacuation. Most important of all for the navy, one Spanish cruiser, the *Reina Mercedes*, remained in the harbor. That night, the Spanish decided to block the harbor they had so assiduously attempted to keep open when Hobson had brought in the *Merrimac*. The *Reina Mercedes* steamed to the channel entrance and was scuttled. In the process, the *Massachusetts* and the *Texas* opened up on her, and the *Mercedes* too failed to block the channel. This brief action completed the destruction of Cervera's ill-fated squadron.

With the Spanish fleet a mass of twisted and smouldering metal, General Shafter generously entered into an armistice with the Spanish commander in order to avoid

further bloodshed. The armistice remained in effect until
July 17, when the Spanish surrendered to Admiral Sampson in Santiago. The Cuban action was over.

The American fleet was ordered to prepare to cross
the Atlantic to deal with the remaining Spanish warships,
including Spain's sole battleship. The Americans were to
engage the Spanish fleet on the Iberian coast or follow
it through the Mediterranean and the Suez Canal if the
Spaniards should attempt to relieve Manila by this route.
The American ships were divided into two squadrons, the
Eastern Squadron, which would go all the way to Manila
if necessary, and the Covering Squadron, which was prepared to escort the first squadron across the Atlantic and
through the Mediterranean and then stay in those waters
to protect the Eastern Squadron's flank and rear. Commodore Watson shifted his broad pennant from the
*Newark* to the *Oregon* and took command of the Eastern
Squadron.

The preparations proved to be unnecessary. Peace
negotiations had begun with the fall of Santiago, and, on
August 7, the Spanish accepted the American surrender
terms. The war was over on August 12, and the United
States of America had become a world power with an empire in the Caribbean and the Pacific.

But Captain Clark had fallen seriously ill with a
tropical fever. The continuous stress of the long and ten-
sion-ridden voyage around South America, the intense
heat of tropical blockade duty, and the final strain of
battle had broken Clark's health. The shocked and sad-
dened men of the *Oregon* learned that, although both had
seemed indestructible, their good ship was stronger than
their plucky fifty-four-year-old skipper.

On August 6, 1898, Captain Albert S. Barker, U.S.N.,
again took command of the *Oregon*, and Clark was ordered home on the *St. Louis* for medical treatment. In his
modest autobiography, written twenty years later, Clark
recalled his departure from the *Oregon*:

There are a few occasions in a man's life which will remain with him always. . . . One . . . I can never forget was the day when, broken in health, I left the *Oregon*. It was a pleasure to find that the boat in which I was to be rowed to the northbound steamer was manned by my officers. That is an honor deeply appreciated by any captain. But I was surprised and hurt, as we left the ship's side, that none of the men were visible. Suddenly, as if moved by one spring, they rose from the decks where they had been lying concealed, and led by old Murphy, the chief boatswain's mate, joined in a ringing shout of "God bless our captain." So the last impression I had of the *Oregon*, as we rowed away, was a forest of waving arms and tossing caps, seen through a mist, although the day was clear and bright.[1]

When the people of the state of Oregon learned of the victory at Santiago and of Clark's illness, a subscription was taken up to buy him a gold sword. The precious weapon was manufactured in Portland and sent to Clark with the admiration and gratitude of the people of the state.

Clark recovered but never saw sea duty again. In March, 1899, he was assigned command of the navy yard at League Island. It was not until 1901 that the Navy recognized his distinguished service on the *Oregon* by advancing him six numbers on the captains list "for eminent and conspicuous conduct in battle." His next billet was as governor of the naval home in Washington, D.C. Finally, on June 16, 1902, four years after Santiago, he was promoted to rear admiral. His last assignment was as the president of the Naval Examination and Retirement Boards in Washington, from which he retired himself on August 4, 1905.

The *Oregon*'s great commander lived with his granddaughter in California until his death in 1922 at the age of seventy-nine. Toward the end, the aged hero was little remembered by any save his old shipmates. In 1915, as the Panama Canal neared completion, there had been talk of having Clark take command of the *Oregon* once more, with as many of the old *Oregon* hands as could be mustered, and traverse the canal to officially open the waterway inspired by the ship's great race. But the trip never took place. The Great War in Europe had darkened all festivities, and the Spanish-American War seemed almost as distant and forgotten as the Second Punic War. Clark, however, died as he lived, a man without bitterness, glad to have had the opportunity to serve his beloved country.

On August 14, 1898, the *New York*, the *Brooklyn*, the *Iowa*, the *Massachustts*, the *Indiana*, and the *Oregon* weighed anchor and departed Cuban waters at long last. The victorious battle squadron headed for New York City and arrived there on August 20 to a tumultuous victory celebration. Arranged in line of column order, the vessels steamed into New York Harbor, all flags flying, whistles shrieking, and surrounded by harbor craft, pleasure boats, and sail. The sailors were given their long awaited and much deserved liberty, and there was hardly a jack among them who had to buy his own drinks that week in Old New York.

It was time for the *Oregon*'s long-neglected overhaul. Over a year had passed since the ship was last in dry dock, and her hull was foul with tons of barnacles, seaweed, and other debris that had accumulated in the tropical waters off Cuba. Therefore, Captain Barker ordered the ship into the Brooklyn Navy Yard, where the overhaul began on August 20. There, hundreds of people visited the vessel daily.

Meanwhile, affairs were not going so smoothly in the new American empire. To the surprise of the American people, the Filipinos had no desire to see their hated Spanish masters merely replaced by American masters. The United States Army commander in the Philippines, Maj. Gen. Wesley Merritt, U.S.A., and the naval leader Admiral Dewey had their hands full with the guerrillas under Emilio Aguinaldo. The unfortunate war against the people of the Philippines would go on for three years.

Dewey asked the Navy Department to reinforce his squadron at Manila, and the department agreed. The admiral was less concerned with Filipino military activities than with the possibility of foreign—particularly German —intervention in the islands. He wanted the fabulous *Oregon,* and he got her.

The ship was painted peacetime white once more. The naval militiamen were detached and sent home with the thanks and good wishes of the navy and their regular navy shipmates. Some men whose enlistments had expired took their discharges and returned to civilian life. Still others left the *Oregon* through routine transfers of personnel. Always with ships and men, the faces change one by one until all are different, but the ship and the spirit live on.

On October 12, 1898, the *Oregon* was underway once more. She headed for the Pacific via the Strait of Magellan in company with the *Iowa,* the supply ship *Celtic,* the collier *Scindia,* and the distilling ship *Iris.* Captain Barker was senior officer present afloat for the expedition.

The cruise to the Pacific was more leisurely than the *Oregon*'s previous race to the Atlantic. The *Oregon* and the *Iowa* arrived in Rio de Janeiro in time to participate in festivities celebrating the anniversary of the founding of the Republic of Brazil. Then the vessels rounded the tip of South America and headed for Callao, Peru, where they received a resounding welcome on December 12. The *Iowa* then headed north to San Francisco for repairs. The collier and the supply ship had been detached previously, and so only the *Oregon* and the *Iris* were left for the journey to Manila. They arrived there at sunset on March 18, 1899. A Navy band from Dewey's squadron hailed the vessels with "The Star-Spangled Banner" as they glided to anchor firing their salutes to the revered admiral.

The *Oregon* had once more performed superbly underway, making the journey without any engineering difficulty and arriving in perfect condition. Dewey cabled the Navy Department, "The *Oregon* and the *Iris* arrived today. The *Oregon* is in fit condition for any duty."

The beleaguered naval officer—who was administering a large city and an enormous colony and fending off foreign sharks—was delighted to have the *Oregon* at his side. She was the first battleship assigned to his Asiatic Squadron. All his other major ships, including the *Olympia*, were of course only cruisers. The *Oregon* relieved the *Olympia* as flagship. Captain Barker wrote Secretary of the Navy John D. Long that Dewey was at last confident that no foreign power would dare to attack the Philippines. One battleship had shifted the balance of power in the Far Pacific.

On November 7, the *Oregon* joined a squadron that landed General Wheaton in Lingayen Gulf and on the fifteenth, she supported a column of troops sent north along the shore. Then she attacked Vigan, some hundred miles to the north, at the request of General Young; on the twenty-sixth, she landed a party of sailors and marines under Commander McCracken to seize the port.

The annexation of the Philippines after payments to Spain placed the United States in the midst of the Far East trade muddle. Anti-Western and antiimperialist resentment was growing in weak, corrupt, and faction-torn China. Russia and Japan were already beginning the light sparring that would lead in 1905 to Japan's knockout victory in the Russo-Japanese War, and the two nations were bent on carving out large pieces of Chinese territory for themselves.

The Chinese people under Boxer leadership rebelled against their own corrupt government and the foreign concessionaires. Peking, including the embassies of the imperialist nations, was quickly placed under siege by the Boxers. In the summer of 1905, the trading nations gathered an invasion army to relieve the city. The *Oregon* was reluctantly detached from Philippine duty to serve as both transport and support ship for the growing American presence in China. She would first sail to Taku and then patrol the China coast.

# 8

# Disaster
# and
# Rescue

The *Oregon*, now under the command of Capt. George F. F. Wilde, U.S.N., made for Hong Kong to pick up extra sailors and marines who had been shipped there previously from Manila and who were needed at Peking. The *Oregon* departed Hong Kong on June 23, 1900, and steamed north towards Taku, the nearest port to Peking. Captain Wilde was under orders to make haste. Unfortunately he took the shortest and least safe route. The *Oregon* rounded the Shantung Peninsula and, on June 28, was about to enter the Gulf of Pechili when Wilde decided to anchor in a dense fog three miles south of Now-Ki Island Light in the Chang-Shan Channel, approximately 38 degrees north latitude and 121 degrees east longitude. The next morning, the weather cleared, and Wilde put two boats over to take soundings. They reported 5½ fathoms in the channel eastward. But the ship was hardly underway when it struck Pinnacle Rock, an obstruction twenty-five feet high and encircled by a shoal. The forward compartment was flooded, the skin of the ship was cut through to frame nineteen along the side, and there were small holes through the bottom. Any rough weather and the *Oregon* was lost.

Despite the fact that it was the stormy season, the weather and the *Oregon*'s luck held good for three key days. Rescue ships rushed to her aid, the vessel was lightened, and temporary repairs were made. The *Oregon* was not to die on that distant Chinese rock. The ship desperately needed dry-docking and major hull repairs, but the nearest American dry dock was of course on the west coast of the United States. The Russian naval facility at Port Arthur was only sixty miles away from where the *Oregon* had been refloated. The Russians, however, declined to help the *Oregon*, stating that their dock was too narrow and that, furthermore, they were too busy to assist. It was the Japanese who came to the rescue. Their cruiser *Akitisushima* was the first foreign vessel to arrive at the scene. Another early arrival was the Chinese cruiser *Mai Chi*, which had been detailed to protect foreigners in the nearby coastal town of Tengchow. The Chinese assistance was outstanding, and, in return for the aid, Wilde permitted the *Mai Chi* to hoist the American flag when threatened with capture by Russian vessels spearheading Russia's expansion of her sphere of influence in North China. Three years later, Peking would formally thank Washington for this protection.

The Japanese were most anxious to help the Americans, especially since the Russians had turned them down. The *Oregon* eased her way slowly out of Chinese waters and limped under escort to the Japanese naval base at Kure. There, the Japanese provided every assistance possible, even though they needed their large dry docks for their own busy vessels. Meanwhile, the *Oregon*'s marine detachment joined the expedition for the relief of Peking.

Capt. Wilde was relieved by Capt. Francis W. Dickins, U.S.N., on February 22, 1901, and on April 7, Capt. Charles M. Thomas, U.S.N., took over command of the *Oregon*. The *Oregon*'s material condition was not perfect even after the dry-docking, and Thomas's orders were to bring his ship home. Preparations were made to sail the Pacific again.

The *Oregon*'s first port of call upon her return home was to be San Francisco. When the people of that city learned that their home-built, world famous battleship was returning for the first time since her great race around South America and her glorious day at Santiago, a massive celebration was planned for the estimated day of arrival, June 13, 1901. Unfortunately for the city fathers as well as the ship, the *Oregon* steamed into the Golden Gate a full twenty-four hours ahead of schedule. She still was the fastest American battleship afloat, perhaps the fastest battleship in the world at that time. In spite of the *Oregon*'s early arrival, the San Franciscans celebrated her return. They especially honored her great builders, the men of the Union Iron Works, eventually to be the Bethlehem Steel Company's Shipbuilding Division. From San Francisco, the *Oregon* steamed north to the Bremerton Navy Yard once more. There she was laid up in ordinary and refitted.

By 1902, tensions were mounting in the Far East. China's government was disintegrating because of internal problems as well as external pressures from the voracious trading powers, particularly Russia and Japan. The *Oregon* was put back into commission and sailed for the China Sea under the command of Capt. Joseph Giles Easton U.S.N., to commence four years of showing the flag and supporting American "interests" in China.

On February 8, 1904, the Imperial Japanese Navy attacked the Imperial Russian Fleet at Chemulpo without warning, and the Russo-Japanese War was on. The *Oregon* was involved in one incident during the conflict. Anchored off Shanghai one evening under the command of Capt. John P. Merrell, U.S.N., she watched Japanese destroyers chase the Russian warship *Askold* into the bay. The bay formed a part of neutral Chinese waters, and the Russian ship was theoretically safe, but the Japanese had little respect for such niceties and deployed for a torpedo attack. Captain Merrell ordered the *Oregon*'s searchlights turned on the Japanese destroyers, and the lights blinded and confused the Japanese long enough to allow the Russian ship to escape up the river. The Japanese protested this violation of international law in illuminating their vessels. Merrell growled back that he would turn more than lights on them if they did not respect the neutrality of the port. The thirteen-inch guns of the Bulldog of the Navy could still bite.

Anti-American sentiment in China was on the rise, partly due to the general hatred of the exploiting "foreign devils," but mostly due to the exclusion of Chinese immigrants from the United States, a policy that clearly implied prejudice. On July 20, 1905, Chinese Nationalists instituted a boycott of American goods in Shanghai. The boycott was successful and quickly spread through all of South China, then to the Philippines, Hawaii, and even to the Japanese ports. American businessmen roared for protection. President Theodore Roosevelt on November 15 ordered the Secretary of the Navy to concentrate "as strong a naval force as possible" off China. Preparations were also made for an Army expedition of fifteen thousand troops. The Chinese would buy our goods or else.

Therefore, in February, 1906, the *Oregon* was belligerently patroling off Hong Kong while the American gunboat *El Cano* was steaming on the Yangtze River. On February 26, Roosevelt submitted a set of humiliating demands to the Imperial Chinese Government. The Emperor gave in and issued an edict forbidding expressions of antiforeign sentiments by his subjects everywhere. Unfortunately, the United States had learned how to use gunboat diplomacy.

Now Merrell could bring the *Oregon* home again, and the ship was placed out of commission at the Bremerton

Navy Yard once more. She stayed there for five years, from April 26, 1906, to April 26, 1911. The navy had less need for the *Oregon* than formerly. Newer battleships, more heavily armed, more heavily gunned, were coming into commission as the United States began to build a world fleet. Significantly, the *Oregon* was out of commission during the voyage of the Great White Fleet.

After the *Oregon* was put back in commission, under the command of Capt. Charles F. Pond. U.S.N., she rejoined the now formidable Pacific Fleet. But the *Oregon* was now too old-fashioned to be part of the battle fleet. Her role was merely supportive. She was a famous ship, and others were proud to stand in company with her, but her fighting days seemed over.

The years washed by. Theodore Roosevelt's great strategic dream, the Panama Canal, was soon to open. Many Americans felt it would be a grand, sentimental gesture to have the *Oregon*, manned by her Spanish-American War crew under old Admiral Clark, sail first through the canal. In June, 1913, sixty thousand state of Oregon schoolchildren petitioned President Wilson to allow "their ship," the *Oregon*, to lead the parade through the new waterway. But when the canal opened in 1914, the terrible war in Europe prevented large-scale celebrations. No one was in much of a mood to celebrate any international event when Europe was tearing herself to bits and millions of humans were slaughtering one another.

The opening of the Panama-Pacific Exposition at San Francisco in 1915 found the *Oregon* on duty in the Golden Gate under the command of Comdr. Joseph M. Reeves, U.S.N., who later became an admiral. Reeves had served as assistant engineer in the port engineroom in 1898. Thousands of fair goers visited the old war relic. The *Oregon* was still the most famous ship in the navy. In 1916, the entire United States Pacific Fleet passed in review for the second year of the exposition, and the *Oregon*, under Comdr. G. W. Williams, U.S.N., served as reviewing ship.

After the United States entered World War I, the *Oregon*, under command of Comdr. C. P. Snyder, U.S.N., was ordered once more to the Bremerton Navy Yard. The vessel was overhauled and modernized at a cost of $1 million and then had a short wartime career as a west coast training vessel, providing training and experience in navigation, seamanship, and gunnery for officers and men soon to be assigned to combat ships in the war zones. For part of this time, the *Oregon* served as designated flagship of the Pacific Fleet.

A unique assignment came to the *Oregon* with the Bolshevik Revolution and Russia's withdrawal from the world war. The *Oregon* was selected as an escort vessel for an expedition of American troops to Siberia. The men, under Gen. William Sidney Graves, U.S.A., joined with other allied forces, ostensibly to try to prevent Allied war supplies in Russia from falling into German hands, but actually to help White Russian counterrevolutionaries. America's "Siberian adventure" has been long forgotten by Americans and long remembered by the Russians. The expedition failed, and the Allied troops withdrew, the Japanese most reluctantly. They had sent the largest number of troops and had the most to gain by maintaining a military presence in Siberia.

After returning to the United States, the *Oregon*, under Lt. Comdr. W. E. Madden, U.S.N., was temporarily placed out of commission on June 16, 1919, after two thirds of her crew were attacked by influenza during the terrible epidemic of April, 1919.

On August 21, 1919, the *Oregon* was once more taken out of the reserve fleet and put back into commission to serve as the reviewing ship when President Woodrow Wilson and the Secretary of the Navy Josephus Daniels gave a postwar welcome to the Pacific Fleet under Adm. Hugh Rodman, U.S.N., at Seattle. A bronze tablet was placed on the deck where the president had stood during the review. The use of the *Oregon* as reviewing vessel was a sentimental gesture, for the Navy had long realized that the fighting days of the old ship were over and her military value in the age of the fifteen-inch-gun dreadnaught was nil. The *Oregon* was decommissioned for the last time on October 4, 1919. Her final commanding officer was Capt. I. C. Wettengill, U.S.N.

It was planned that the old Spanish-American War battleships *Oregon*, *Indiana*, *Iowa*, and *Massachusetts* be used for target practice and sunk at sea. However, the United Spanish War Veterans and other civic organizations mounted a campaign to save the *Oregon*. In 1920, they won temporary success when that great naval buff, Assistant Secretary of the Navy Franklin D. Roosevelt, intervened and the *Oregon* alone of the old battleships survived the gunfire and scrap heap.

Under the terms of the Washington Conference on Limitation of Armaments, 1921–22, the *Oregon* was again scheduled for the scrap yard. If the United States were to limit its number of battleships, then "BB3" could not be an old Spanish-American War relic. Again the public uproar commenced, this time louder and clearer. The people of the state of Oregon particularly wanted the old ship saved, and they wanted her nearby so that their children could see the proud old conqueror and walk her decks.

In 1925, the state of Oregon officially petitioned the United States Government to have the vessel preserved as a memorial and berthed in Portland. Oregon governor Ben Wilson Olcott personally wrote to the Navy Department requesting that the plea of the state legislature be granted. He pledged that the state would live up to any agreement the Navy might require, including a guarantee that adequate sums would be appropriated annually for the maintenance and preservation of the *Oregon* Memorial.

The Navy Department agreed at last, with the proviso that the state create an acceptance fund to maintain the vessel in a condition that would safely allow visitors to board her. The legislature of the state of Oregon enacted a law creating a permanent *Oregon* fund. The veteran would be brought to Portland.

At Bremerton, the propeller shaft of the *Oregon* was cut in two, and the engines were dismantled. Then, with a regular navy crew aboard and commanded by Capt. Robert T. Menner, U.S.N., the old ship was pushed and pulled by navy tugs down Puget Sound and out into the Pacific. At the mouth of the Columbia River, she was met by the veteran pilots Capt. O. P. Rankin and Capt. N. Hampson, who took command of the *Oregon* and the navy tugs on their trip up the Columbia and Willamette rivers. The *Oregon* was flying the old "homeward bound" pennant for the last time. Just below Portland, she was boarded by the queen of the 1925 Rose Festival and her court. The reception given the old ship on her arrival at a berth at the east end of Portland's Broadway Bridge was glorious and long remembered. Her arrival officially opened the 1925 Rose Festival.

State officials signed for the ship when she arrived in Portland on July 14, 1925. She had been officially accepted from the Navy Department, represented by Captain Menner, on July 3, 1925, the anniversary of the Battle of Santiago, by Gov. Walter M. Pierce on behalf of the people of the state of Oregon.

Some years before, on May 8, 1919, the ship's newspaper, *The Bull Dog*, had summed up the bluejackets' feeling about the ship:

> She's been sailing the seas for Uncle Sam since 1896, and in that time she has won a name as one of the historic ships of the Navy. At present it seems as though her days are numbered. There is a newspaper report that she is to continue in service with the Pacific Fleet, but our orders to return to Bremerton and put "The Bull Dog" in a comfortable kennel for a long rest have not been revoked at this writing. But whether she keeps on sailing or ties up in the Navy Yard, we'll say that we are proud to have had duty aboard her. It is a privilege to serve on a ship with such a record and it will be a distinction to boast of in the future years when one reads in history of the good old *OREGON* who romped around the Horn and fought the good fight to victory at Santiago, that we

once swung our hammocks between her decks. In this war she was too old to be in the first line but she guarded the nation on this coast, has trained many gun crews who peppered the suds with accurate fire from the decks of ships which carried our men and the necessary food and gear to France, and has sent out many sons with commissions to serve on other ships and to command sub-chasers, and she is winding up her duty in this war with this important mission to boost the Victory Loan on the West Coast that Uncle Sam may pay his debts and go forward to new achievements to peace as important as his glorious accomplishments in war.

So, once again, "Here's to the grand old *OREGON*."

# 9

# Fiasco
# and
# Final Glory

In 1925, the governor of the state of Oregon appointed a commission of five members to manage the affairs of the battleship *Oregon*. The original members of the commission were Col. Carle Abrams, Col. U. G. Worrell (retired), and Howard Waddell, all veterans of the Spanish-American War and World War I; Lafe Manning, a Spanish-American War veteran who had seen service on the battleship; and Mrs. Cora A. Thompson, wife of a Spanish-American War veteran. In 1928, Mrs. Thompson resigned from the commission to assume the duties of secretary and business manager of the battleship commission.

The possibility of establishing a National War Museum aboard the ship was taken up by the Battleship *Oregon* Commission in August, 1925, and Mrs. Thompson was placed in charge of this work. Progress was slow until 1928, when the United Spanish War Veterans, at their national encampment in Havana, Cuba, passed a resolution instructing each state department of the organization to send all its members a request for gifts and loans to the museum. The following year, the National Auxiliary, United Spanish War Veterans, passed a similar resolution. Then material began to arrive, not only from the United States but also from England and Canada.

The old warship became very much a part of the civic structure of the city of Portland. Various organizations, such as the Boy Scouts, held meetings aboard, and schoolchildren scurried through the ship on fall and spring outings. It was a good fate and a good life for a retired old veteran, but bleak days were approaching.

In 1938, the Battleship *Oregon* Commission sponsored a project that would have saved the vessel from its later, ignominious fate, had the plans been carried to completion. The idea was to dig a short channel shoreward, warp the old ship in, and permanently encase it in concrete at a place to be called the Battleship *Oregon* Marine Park. The *Oregon* would be the historic jewel in a recreational setting. Unfortunately, Portland and the state of Oregon were too enmeshed in the struggle with the Great Depression to provide funds for the entire worthwhile project, but the ship was at least moved to safer quarters. That year, the United Spanish War Veterans held their national convention in Portland, and one of the ceremonies was the towing of the old battleship from the northeast end of the Broadway Bridge to the southwest end of the Hawthorne Bridge. There the *Oregon* was floated in a basin roughly carved from the bank and bed of the Willamette River, completely out of danger from the regular channel traffic. Later in the day, the basin and the site of the future Battleship *Oregon* Marine Park were dedicated.

A few months later, the public-spirited citizens of Portland and the state raised enough money to complete the basin and a seawall, lay out the park, and build a long, solidly railed gangplank from street level to the deck of the battleship.

But the *Oregon*, unfortunately, was still afloat, still movable, and worst of all, still in the possession of the federal government. She was still officially only on loan to the people of the state of Oregon.

Now begins the mystery and embarrassment of a great ship's demise through misplaced patriotic zeal, stupidity, avarice, and indifference. Almost immediately after the Japanese attack on Pearl Harbor, the governor of Oregon, Charles A. Sprague, who obviously knew little about modern naval warfare, offered to return the *Oregon* to the navy so that she might serve for "coastal or other defense use." The offer, although generous and high minded, was absurd. The *Oregon* had no military value whatsoever. The navy at first declined the offer, indicating rightly that the historical importance of the *Oregon* outweighed any possible operational value the ship might have. Still, rumors of her imminent scrapping began to circulate widely, and patriotic organizations deluged the navy with letters and petitions of protest over such a fate for the vessel.

On September 15, 1942, the beleaguered Navy Department released to the nation a statement headlined, "Navy Knows of No Plans to Scrap USS *Oregon*." The statement read in part, " ... the maintenance of this historic shrine remindful of the resourcefulness, perseverance and loyalty of the old Navy remains an inspiration to our fighting forces." Fine words, but a bundle of lies, for plans had indeed been laid to scrap the *Oregon*. The United States War Production Board, zealously and sometimes fanatically searching for scrap steel to feed the voracious and insatiable furnaces of war production, had eyed the ship. Knowing that the navy would soon be forced to reverse its decision concerning the ship, Under Secretary of the Navy James Forrestal informed Governor Sprague that, due to the "great necessity for scrap metal and the pressure exerted upon us to make every possible contribution toward the building up of an adequate stockpile, this decision will probably have to be reconsidered."[1]

The matter was referred to President Franklin D. Roosevelt. The president surely felt bad about the situation. He was a naval buff and an amateur historian. Furthermore, he had helped to save the *Oregon* after World War I. Finally, Roosevelt wrote to Secretary of the Navy Frank Knox:

> The White House
>
> October 26, 1942
>
> Dear Colonel Knox:
>
> It is with great reluctance that I authorize the Navy Department to turn the USS *Oregon* over to the War Production Board for reduction to scrap metal.
>
> It is my understanding that the Department will take immediate action toward the preservation of the USS *Olympia* as a naval relic of the Spanish-American war period.
>
> Sincerely yours,
>
> Franklin D. Roosevelt

Even the *Olympia*, as it turned out, was not preserved by the navy. Dewey's flagship was finally saved by the continuing efforts of private charity. Knox was clearly not surprised at Roosevelt's decision. In fact, he had anticipated it, for, on October 24, he had written a letter to a group of concerned *Oregon* supporters—the Battleship *Oregon* Naval Post No. 1478, Veterans of Foreign Wars—stating somewhat fatuously that: "despite the fact that I, like yourselves, would like to preserve the *Oregon*, the necessity for utilizing all available strategic material makes it imperative that the metals of the *Oregon* be utilized. Far from being scrapped, the strategic materials of the *Oregon* will be reclaimed and converted into war material, and thereby again join in battle, a choice I am sure the good ship would make, were it within her power to do so."

With almost immodest haste, Knox had the vessel stricken from the navy list and put up for sale on November 2, just a few days after he received the president's letter. The business of her sale proceeded circumspectly. Special invitations were sent out to those selected to bid for her scrapping contract. These invitations stated somewhat mysteriously that "due to the fact that this ship is of inestimable sentimental value, bidding and award of this ship for scrapping will not be handled under the usual circumstances. . . . Award will be predicated not only upon the highest bid, but also upon other factors which will be discussed with the bidders at the opening of bids on board the vessel."

These "factors" were never defined. Only the single military mast of the *Oregon* was allowed to be saved, and it is all that remains of the ship today. It occupies a place of honor on the Portland seawall. On December 7, 1942, (O Irony!) the old ship was knocked down for only $35,000 to two Portland businessmen, Edwin M. Ricker and William O. McKay. The *Oregon* was towed to Kalama, Wash. Work on the ship began almost immediately, and it seemed at first that her steel might indeed make its tiny contribution to the war effort. However, steel scrap became less and less critical, and the dismantling slowed down. The navy yard at Mare Island, Calif., became interested in some of the *Oregon*'s machinery, and, for a while, there were some negotiations between the yard and the wreckers.

As September, 1943, began, only the superstructure and internal machinery had been removed from the vessel. Concerned citizens and navy historians were totally disgusted with what by then appeared to be either vandalism or crude wartime speculation and profiteering. The navy was extremely embarrassed and stopped the little work being done on the dismantling project. The ship was requisitioned back from her owners. The *Oregon* was not officially returned to the navy list, for such action would have been absurd, but she was again referred to by her previous designation, IX-22. The IX stood for *miscellaneous vessel,* a designation given to such historic ships as the *Constitution* and the *Constellation.*

The navy decided that there was still some military use in the *Oregon* after all, although not of course as a combat vessel. The American island-hopping campaign in the Pacific was proceeding apace, and a vessel was needed to carry blasting material and ammunition out to Guam and store the explosives. The *Oregon* was going to war again. Her armored hull was perfect for dynamite stowage and so she was ballasted with gravel and loaded with 1,400 tons of explosives. The seabees were waiting for her on Guam.

In July, 1944, the *Oregon* was on the high seas, under tow this time, back in those familiar Pacific waters. She was taken to Port Merizo, where Japanese stragglers took her under fire one evening. The seabees continued the work of blasting and harbor clearing. Each day, the commander of Service Squadron 12, to which the *Oregon* was assigned, would send LCT's and LCVP's alongside for loads of dynamite, which were then transported to Apra Harbor, Tinian, Saipan, or Palau. The LCI(G)474 served as the *Oregon*'s permanent tender.

The *Oregon* was moored at Port Merizo for safety's sake, to keep the floating bomb away from more populated areas. But the crew who worked aboard the *Oregon* did not feel much danger, for they assumed that, with prescribed precautions, no serious accidents would result. Hourly temperature readings were taken in the holds, windscopes were rigged for circulation of air through all hatches, and of course no smoking was allowed on the ship. Armed guards were maintained on the bow and stern of the old battleship and heavy use was made of searchlights at night. The work was done at night because the extremely hot weather made work on the steel decks unbearable during the day. Each night, about fifteen tons of dynamite were unloaded from the ship. The boxes were brought up from the holds to the main deck by a deck winch and then sent down a chute to the landing craft.

During the stay at Port Merizo, part of the ship's work consisted of establishing good will among the native inhabitants. The village of Merizo had about five hundred Chamorro people. When the *Oregon* first arrived, many of the villagers began coming out to the ship, anxious to talk to the men and tell of their experiences during the Japanese occupation of the island. It was against the rules to provide civilians large quantities of food, but they were given small rations of flour and other baking materials, and some of the men also provided the Chamorros with clothing. The village had a grade school with a principal and four teachers. All the boys of the school belonged to Boy Scout troops, and the boatswain's mate and the signalman were assigned to spend spare moments instructing the scouts in handling lines, tying various knots, and signaling with flags and blinkers. One of the officers began instructing the teachers on the U.S. government and the Constitution. The Chamorros were welcome guests, and it was not unusual to have about ten to fifteen at the mess. A small native orchestra, which had two violins, a banjo, and a ukelele, often came out to the ship on Sundays after divine services on the island. The Chamorros were invited to the services. At first, only the women attempted to join in the religious songs, but, on succeeding Sundays, more and more Chamorros learned the words and melodies. It was not long before every man, woman, and child sang without hesitation and with full confidence. For better or for worse, the *Oregon* had brought American civilization back to Port Merizo.

As the fighting passed to the east, the islands that had been dearly won in American blood grew less and less important until even Guam became a backwater to the war. All the *Oregon*'s dynamite and ammunition had been requisitioned, and she languished and rusted in the now almost silent harbor of Port Merizo.

After the war ended, the *Oregon* was placed under the jurisdiction of the commanding officer of the Naval Operations Base, Apra, who had no idea what to do with the ship. There was some talk of sinking her to form part of a breakwater, but nothing ever came of the plan.

Then, on November 14, 1948, Hurricane Agnes ravaged the Marianas. Fifty-knot winds and high seas pounded and tore at the old ship until, in torment, she broke free from her moorings, and unmanned, moved swiftly out to sea. The dawn of November 16 found the hurricane blown out and the *Oregon* out of sight and presumably resting peacefully on the bottom of the Pacific Ocean. However, search planes were dispatched just to make sure the old relic was not still afloat and menacing the sea lanes.

On December 8, 1948, a very surprised naval aviator spotted a great steel hull seemingly underway, five hundred miles southeast of Guam and heading for the Philippines. The *Oregon* had simply taken a month's unauthorized leave to pay a last visit to some of her old haunts.

Hastily, the commanding officer at Guam dispatched a fleet tug to lasso the AWOL and tow her home to Apra Harbor. He then reported that the ship had suffered "no apparent damage during unscheduled voyage."

In the United States, the *Oregon*'s escapade once more drew attention to her existence. Many people who had once been interested in the vessel had forgotten her, but the solo voyage reminded them that she was still alive. Oregon legislators, particularly United States Senator Wayne Morse, remembered all the hot air expended over the *Oregon*'s "noble sacrifice" in 1942 and demanded that the vessel be brought back stateside and restored to her former condition. While this effort was being made, other groups of Americans interested in the historical heritage of their nation were mounting campaigns to save other vessels, including the frigate *Constellation*, which would indeed be saved, and the steam sloop *Hartford*, which would be destroyed.

Alas, the *Oregon* was now almost beyond restoration. In 1953, some people suggested the ship be rehabilitated at Guam, but even this plan proved impractical. All that was left of the old warrior was the hull, with its original steel plates riveted together in San Francisco in the last decade of the nineteenth century. The millions of dollars needed to bring the ship back to her pre-World War II condition would have had to come out of naval appropriations, and the funds could not be spared from a peacetime budget. Still, the cost would not have been more than that of a new jet fighter plane. Finally, Congress decided in the name of the American people. The Eighty-third Congress, in Public Law 523, ordered the Secretary of the Navy to dispose of the *Oregon*. All that her many friends had accomplished in eight years of effort to save her was an ignominious death. They could not even force the government to tow her out to sea and let her sink beneath the waves.

On March 15, 1956, the *Oregon* was sold to the Massey Supply Corporation for $208,000—a considerable hike from the $35,000 the vessel had brought in 1943, when she was in good shape. Massey quickly turned around and resold the hulk to the Iwai Sanggo Company, a Japanese scrap and salvage firm. The Japanese sent a tug to Guam, made fast their towing cables, and dragged the hull to Kawasaki, Japan, where the ship was quickly broken up and her pieces were fed into the giant steel mills of Japan.

In some ways, the former enemy was kinder to the ship than her own people had been, for just inside the main gate of the Yokosuka Naval Base of the Japanese Maritime Defense Force may be found some anchor links from an old, old ship and a plaque with this inscription in Japanese and English:

IN MEMORY OF A GALLANT SHIP
U.S.S. OREGON
1896–1919

This section of anchor chain from the historic U.S.S. Oregon was presented to the U.S. Naval Base at

Yokosuka, Japan, through the generosity of Ryozo Hiranuma, the Mayor of Yokohama, in cooperation with Lionel M. Summers U.S. Consulate General, Yokohama. Presented 26 February, 1957.

And thus lived and died McKinley's Bulldog, the battleship *Oregon*. She was born in an exuberant America that was just beginning to turn its eyes from the closed frontier and the problems of internal expansion to the heady, dangerous dreams of colonialism and world power. The ship was superbly built and gave tribute to American technological progress and the growth of heavy industry in California. In war, no American vessel ever served her country better. In peace, she showed the flag, trained thousands of naval officers and enlisted men (several of whom went on to distinguished and formative military careers), and then was a floating historical museum. Except for the *Constitution*, no ship has been more revered and loved by the American people.

The *Oregon* died in a period of post-Korean War disenchantment with things military, although in truth she had been needlessly ruined by misguided patriotism during World War II. The old lady should have been allowed to live. Her inspiration is sorely needed now and will be needed even more in the future. But, surely, she has a secure place in history and in the heart of any American who has ever read of the great race around Cape Horn and the chase of the *Cristobal Colon*.

# Appendix A

## U.S.S. *Oregon's* Characteristics at Commissioning

The hull of the *Oregon* was protected at the waterline by belts of the strongest available armor, 18 inches thick. The belts rose 3 feet above the water and extended to a depth of 4½ feet below the water. They turned in forward and aft to sweep around the oases of the armored redoubts. The armored area accounted for about 75 percent of the water plane. The belts were backed by 6 inches of wood, two ¾-inch steel plates, and a 10-foot belt of coal. Forward and abaft of the side armor belts were heavy underwater protective decks that sloped at the sides to 4½ feet below the water. Over the armor belt was an armored deck that had belts of water-excluding material worked on its slopes. Above the belt armor and from redoubt to redoubt, the sides were protected by 5 inches of steel.

The vessel was cut sharp up forward, making a powerful ram bow and doing away with excessive bow waves on account of the easier lines so obtained. This feature aided greatly the maneuverability of the ship.

Below the waterline, the *Oregon's* bow swept forward to form a pointed ram. Above the ram, the bow was pierced for a surface torpedo tube. At the level of the deck, the bow bore a striped red, white, and blue shield. On billboards on each side of the forecastle rested a bower and a sheet anchor, whose chains were led through hawse pipes to a steam winch just forward of the huge forward thirteen-inch gun turret. The anchor davits and two ventilators, all of which could be unshipped when clearing for action, and a scuttle were also located in the bow.

Rising from the waterline belt at each end of the ship were armored redoubts made of steel 17 inches thick. These redoubts extended above the main deck 3½ feet and gave an armored freeboard of 15 feet 2 inches. They protected the turning gear of the turrets and all the operations of loading. The turrets were designed to be inclined. They were 17 inches thick and were powerfully strengthened. The horizontal thickness of the inclined turrets was 20 inches. The conning tower had armor 10 inches thick; a tube of 7-inch thickness protected the voice pipes, electric wires, and steering connections.

The battery of the *Oregon* was made up of four thirteen-inch breechloading rifles, eight eight-inch breechloading rifles, four six-inch breechloading rifles, twenty six-pounder rapid-fire guns, two Gatlings, and six torpedo tubes. The Navy Department believed that this battery represented a weight of armament superior to that of any battleship laid down by a foreign power.

The thirteen-inch guns were nearly eighteen feet above the water and had large arcs of train. The six-inch guns were almost fifteen feet above the water and fired across the center line of the ship. The eight-inch guns were mounted across the middle line of the ship. All these guns could pierce at two miles the armor of many of the best armored cruisers and could also be used with great effect against the lightly armored and unarmored parts of a heavier battleship. The guns could be brought into action early in an engagement, on account of their great height. The guns of the powerful secondary battery were so disposed that a stream of projectiles might radiate from the vessel. Such a stream would lead to the almost certain destruction of any light boat venturing within range.

Fixed torpedo tubes were carried at the bow and stern and two training tubes, firing through five inches of protection, were carried on each broadside.

The 8-inch guns had barbettes made of steel 10 inches thick, inclined turrets of 8½-inch thickness, and cone bases and loading tubes of 3-inch thickness. The 6-inch guns were protected by 5 inches of armor. Ammunition was sent up inside 2-inch splinter bulkheads worked around the deck of these guns. Some of the six-pounder guns were mounted between decks and had 2-inch armor worked around them. Other six-pounders were exposed and had the usual service shields. The one-pounder guns were protected by 2 inches of steel.

The navy had paid special attention to the ammunition and had secured a rapid, efficient, and thoroughly protected supply that was believed to represent an advance upon all systems then in vogue.

Great care had been taken to dispose the *Oregon's* great battery so that one gun might not interfere with the line of fire of another. In addition the small boats had been stowed amidships, where the blasts could not reach them. The sides and decks had been especially strengthened so as to withstand the great strains brought upon them by the fire of the larger guns. The thirteen-inch guns were kept six feet above the deck at the middle line so as to reduce strain on the deck.

The *Oregon* carried a seventy-foot, conical military mast, which rose above the conning tower. This mast carried two tops for rapid-fire and machine guns. The ammunition was sent up to the tops inside the mast. The military mast was surmounted by a tall signal mast, and the enclosed pilot house and signal bridge stood at the foot of the military mast. Aft of the mast were two funnels some forty feet high, with two boat cranes and an array of ventilators between them.

The engines of the ship were of a twin screw, vertical, triple expansion, direct acting, inverted cylinder type. The engines were placed in water-tight compartments and separated by bulkheads. The diameters of the cylinders were: high pressure, 34½ inches; intermediate, 48 inches; low pressure, 75 inches; stroke, 42 inches.

The condensers were of composition and sheet brass, each main condenser having a cooling surface of 6,353 square feet. The circulating pumps were centrifugal and independent. There were four double-ended and two single-ended auxiliary steel boilers of the horizontal return fire-tube type. The main boilers were about 15 feet in outside diameter and 18 feet long. The auxiliary single-ended boilers were about 10 feet 2 inches in diameter and 8½ feet long.

The *Oregon's* bunkers carried 1,800 tons of coal which, it was calculated, would permit her to cruise 16,000 nautical miles at a speed of ten knots. Her crew would consist of 30 officers and 438 men.

# Appendix B

**The Officers of the Oregon during the Race around the Horn.**

Captain ................C. E. Clark
Lieutenant Commander...J. K. Cogswell
Lieutenants ............R. F. Nicholson, W. H. Allen,
                        A. A. Ackerman
Lieutenant junior grade ..E. W. Eberle
Ensigns ................C. L. Hussey, R. Z. Johnston
Captain of Marines ......R. Dickins
Second Lieutenant
   of Marines ...........A. R. Davis
Naval Cadets ...........H. E. Yarnell, L. M.
                        Overstreet, A. G. Magill,
                        C. S. Kempff
Chief Engineer ..........R. W. Milligan
P. A. Engineer ..........C. N. Offley
Asst. Engineers ........J. M. Reeves, F. Lyon
Engineer Cadets ........H. N. Jenson, W. D. Leahy
Surgeon ................P. A. Lovering
Assistant Surgeon .......W. B. Grove
Paymaster ..............S. R. Colhoun

Chaplain ............... P. J. McIntyre
Paymaster's Clerk ....... J. A. Murphy
Boatswain ............. John Costello
Gunner ............... A. S. Williams
Carpenter ............. M. F. Roberts

# Notes

## Chapter 2:  The Launching

1. *San Francisco Chronicle*, 27 October 1893.
2. Ibid.
3. *San Francisco Examiner*, 27 October 1893.

## Chapter 5:  "Six Thousand Miles . . ."

1. Charles Edgar Clark, *My Fifty Years in the Navy*, p. 262.
2. Ibid., p. 270.
3. Ibid., p. 274.
4. Ibid.
5. Ibid.
6. Captain Joshua Slocum, "Sailing Alone Around the World," p. 593.

## Chapter 6:  Into Battle

1. Charles Edgar Clark, *My Fifty Years in the Navy*, pp. 332–333.
2. Ibid., p. 296.
3. Records of the Bureau of Ships, United States Department of the Navy, Washington, D.C.

## Chapter 7:  Mopping Up

1. Charles Edgar Clark, *My Fifty Years in the Navy*, pp. 300–301.

## Chapter 9:  Fiasco and Final Glory

1. John D. Alden, "Whatever Happened to the Battleship *Oregon?*," p. 147.

# Bibliography

Alden, John D. "Whatever Happened to the Battleship *Oregon?" United States Naval Institute Proceedings* 94 (September 1968) :146–149.

Beardsley, C. A., Rear Admiral, U.S.N. "The Trial of the *Oregon." Harper's New Monthly Magazine* 98 (1899) :699–707.

Braisted, William Reynolds. *The United States Navy in the Pacific: 1897–1909.* Austin: University of Texas Press, 1958.

Bryant, Samuel W. *The Sea and the States.* New York: Thomas Y. Crowell Co., 1947.

Cassard, William G. *Battleship* Indiana *and Her Part in the Spanish-American War.* New York, 1898. Compiled and published for the *Indiana* ship's company by Everett B. Mero, chief yeoman, U.S.N.

Clark, Charles E. *My Fifty Years in the Navy.* Boston: Little, Brown & Co., 1917.

Eberle, Lieutenant Edward W., U.S.N. "The *Oregon's* Great Voyage." *Century Magazine* 58 (May–October 1899) : 912–924.

Cannon, Joseph C. *The U.S.S.* Oregon *and the Battle of Santiago.* New York: Comet Press, 1958.

Graves, Major General William S., U.S.A. *America's Siberian Adventure: 1918–1920.* New York: Peter Smith Co., 1941.

Harbaugh, William Henry. *Power and Responsibility: The Life and Times of Theodore Roosevelt.* New York: Farrar, Straus & Cudahy, 1961.

*Harper's Pictorial History of the War with Spain.* New York and London: Harper Brothers, 1899.

Harris, Brayton. *The Age of the Battleship: 1890–1922.* New York: Franklin Watts, 1965.

Hayes, John D. "Admiral Joseph Mason Reeves, U.S.N.: Part I." *Naval War College Review* 23 (November 1970) : 48–57.

Lewis, Charles Lee. *Famous American Naval Officers.* Rev. ed. Boston: L. C. Page, 1945.

Lodge, Henry Cabot. "The Spanish American War." *Harper's New Monthly Magazine* 98 (1899) :449–464, 505–523, 715–733, 833–858.

Mahan, Alfred Thayer. *Lessons of the War with Spain.* 1899. Reprint. Freeport, New York: Books for Libraries Press 1899 ed. 1970.

*New York Times.* 1893–1956.

Puleston, W. D. *Mahan.* New Haven: Yale University Press, 1939.

Sampson, William T. Rear Admiral, U.S.N. "The Atlantic Fleet in the Spanish War." *Century Magazine* 57 (November, 1898–April, 1899), 886–913.

*San Francisco Chronicle.* 1893–1896.

*San Francisco Examiner.* 1893.

Slocum, Captain Joshua, "Sailing Alone Around the World: Being a Personal Narrative of the Experiences of the Sloop 'Spray' on Her Single-Handed Voyage of 46,000 Miles: Part VI, The Homeward Trip from the Cape of Good Hope." *Century Magazine* 59 (February 1900) : 589–600.

Staunton, J. A. "The Naval Campaign of 1898 in the West Indies." *Harper's New Monthly Magazine* 98 (1899) : 175–193.

Wilson, H. W. "The Naval Lessons of the War." *Harper's New Monthly Magazine* 98 (1899) : 288–297.

# Index

Abrams, Col. Carl, 113
Ackerman, Lt. Albert A.,
    52, 126
*Active*, 19
Aguinaldo, Emilio, 100
Ainsworth, Daisy, 16, 20, 22,
    23
*Akitisushima*, 104
*Albatross*, 34
Allen, Lt. W. H., 126
*Amphitrite*, U.S.S., 9, 74
Apra Harbor Naval
    Operations Base, 120
Armor plate, fitting of, 29–30
Army, transportation of the,
    to Cuba, 80
Artic Oil Works, 17
Asiatic Squadron, 102
*Askold*, 106
*Atlanta*, U.S.S., 10

Barker, Capt. Albert S., 44,
    45, 100, 101, 102
    becomes captain of the
    *Oregon*, 98
Battle of Bayamo (1895), 43
Battle of Santiago (1898),
    49, 87–96
Battleship *Oregon*
    Commission, 113, 114

Battleship *Oregon* Naval
    Post No. 1478, Veterans
    of Foreign Wars, 116
Battleships, 5
Bayamo, battle of (1895), 43
*Bay City*, 19
Beardslee, Rear Adm. L. A.,
    31, 33, 34, 36, 37
Bering Sea Patrol, 52
*Bianco Encalada*, 8
*Boston*, U.S.S., 10
Boston Navy Yard, 1
Bostwick, Ens. L. A., 76
Boxer Rebellion, 82, 102
*Bredablik*, 18
Bremerton (Wash.) Navy
    Yard, 47, 69, 105,
    106–7, 108
Bridgetown, Bardados, 66–67
Brinser, H. J., 76
*Brooklyn*, U.S.S., 49, 50, 73,
    76, 78, 83, 86, 88, 89,
    91, 92, 93, 94, 96, 100
Brooklyn Navy Yard,
    overhaul of the *Oregon*
    at, 100
Brown, C. O., 22
Buchanan, Adm. Franklin, 50
Buchanan, James, 42
*Buffalo*, U.S.S., 63

*Bull Dog, The,* quoted,
110–11

Callao, Peru, 56–58
*Calliope,* H.M.S., 12
Campos, Martinez, 43
Carnegie Steel Corporation,
29
*Caroline,* 18
*Castine,* U.S.S., 76
*Celtic,* U.S.S., 101
Cervera y Topete, Adm.
Pascual, 58, 65, 71–75,
76, 89
*Charleston,* U.S.S., viii, 11,
31, 34
Chemulpo, start of
Russo-Japanese War at,
105
*Chicago,* U.S.S., 10
China, service of the *Oregon*
off the coast of, 103–6
Cienfuegos, Cuba, 76
*Cincinnati,* U.S.S., 76
Clark, Capt. Charles Edgar,
31–34, 79–80, 86, 88, 91,
93, 126
career, 48–53
takes command of the
*Oregon,* 55, 56–70
quoted, 92, 98–99
Clark Club, 76
Cogswell, Lt. Comdr. J. K., 126
Colhoun, S. R., 126
*Colorado,* S.S., 52
*Columbia,* U.S.S., 73
Compton, Gen. G., 19, 20
Conger, Benjamin, 17
*Congress,* U.S.S., 8
*Constellation,* U.S.S., 120
*Constitution,* U.S.S. (Old
Ironsides), 48, 122
Cook, Capt. Francis A., 49, 89
*Corwin,* 18

Costello, John, 126
Covering Squadron, 98
Cramp, William, and Sons
Shipyard (Philadelphia),
38
*Cristobal Colon,* 49, 65, 77,
88, 92–95, 122
Cross, R., quoted, 85
Cruisers
armored, 5
protected, 5–6
unprotected, 6
Cuba, attempts by the U.S. to
annex or buy, 41–42
revolutions and guerrilla
warfare in, 42–43
*Cumberland,* U.S.S., 8

Daniels, Josephus, 108
Davis, Lt. A. R., 81, 82, 126
Davis, George T., 51
Davis, Louisa, 51
Destroyers, 6–7
*Detroit,* U.S.S., 74
Dewey, Adm. George, 26, 47,
71, 101
Dickens, Capt. Randolph, 81,
126
Dickie, George, 26
Dickie, James 26
Dickins, Capt. Francis W.,
104–5
*Dictator,* U.S.S., 51
Dolph, Joseph Norton, 16
Dolph, Ruth, 16
*Dolphin,* U.S.S., 10
Donald, W., 26
Donaldson, A., 26
Drake, Lt. Comdr., 39
Dungan, P. B., 76
Dunlap, T. C., 76
*Dupont,* U.S.S., 75

*Eagle,* 76
Eastern Squadron, 98

Easton, Capt. Joseph Giles, 105
Eberle, Lt. E. W., 93, 126
Eckart, William R., 37
*Elath,* 8
*El Cano,* U.S.S., 106
Ellis, Chief Yeoman George, 92
*Enterprise,* U.S.S., 27
Ericsson, John, 8–9
*Ericsson,* U.S.S., 86

Farragut, Adm. David G., 26, 49, 50
*Fearless,* 19
Feldenheimers Silversmiths (Portland, Ore.), 44
Fighting ships, types of, 4–7
First Marine Battalion, 81
First U.S. Volunteer Cavalry (Rough Riders), 80, 83, 85
Fish, Hamilton, 42
Flying Squadron, 73, 74, 77
Forrestal, James, 115
Forsyth, Robert, 26, 35
Frear, Hugo, 26
*Furor,* 88

Garcia, Mario, 43
*Gedney,* 34
*General McDowell,* U.S.S., 18
Gilbert, W. B., 20
*Gloucester,* U.S.S., 86, 88
Gomez, Gen. Maximo, 43
*Governor Markham,* 19
Graves, Gen. William Sidney, 108
Grove, W. B., 126
Guam, liberation of, vii–viii, 118–19
Guantanamo, Cuba, 81–82, 86
Gyroscope, invention of the, 8

Halsey, Adm. William F., Jr., 27

Hampson, Capt. N., 110
Hampton Roads, 59
*Hartford,* U.S.S., 27, 50, 52, 120
Hatch, C. G., 76
Havana, cannonading of (June 26, 1898), 83–85
Hearst, William Randolph, 43
Herbert, Hilary Abner, 16, 30
Hiranuma, Ryozo, 122
*Hist,* 86
Hobson, Lt. Richmond P., 79
Howell, Comdr. J. A., 73
Howison, Capt. Henry L., 19, 39, 40, 44
Hussey, Ens. C. L., 126

*Independence,* U.S.S., 53
*Indiana,* U.S.S., 13, 38, 74, 86, 89, 90, 100, 109
*Infanta Maria Teresa,* 87–90
*Influence of Sea Power upon History* (Mahan), 11
*Iowa,* U.S.S., 74, 75, 76, 80, 86, 89, 100, 101, 109
*Iris,* U.S.S., 101
Iwai Sanggo Company (Japan), 121

Jenson, H. N., 126
*John Adams,* U.S.S., 49
Johnston, Ens. R. Z., 126
Jupiter Inlet, Fla., 69

Kalbfus, C. C., 76
*Katahdin,* 73
Kawasaki, Japan, 121
Kempff, C. S., 126
Key West, Fla., 72, 73
Kinney, Mrs. M. J., 22
Knox, Frank, quoted, 116–17

"Launching of the Oregon" (Simpson), 22
Leahy, Adm. William D., 55, 126

Lee, Gen. Fitzhugh, 46
Long, John D. 47, 102
Longworth, Thomas, 26
Lord, William Paine, 45
Lovering, P. A., 126
Luce, Capt. Stephen B., 49
*Lynch*, H.M.S., 7
Lyon, F., 126

*MacArthur*, U.S.S., 18, 34
McCormick, Capt. Alexander
    H., 45–46, 47, 48
*Macedonian*, U.S.S., 49
Maceo, Antonio, 43
McIntyre, P. J., 126
McKay, James, 26
McKay, William O., 117
McKinley, William, 46
Madden, Lt. Comdr. W. E.,
    108
Magill, A. G., 76, 126
Mahan, Alfred Thayer, 5, 11,
    48, 61, 62, 67, 71
*Mahopac* U.S.S., 52
*Mai Chi*, 104
*Maine*, U.S.S., 11, 57, 58, 72
    destruction of, 46–47
Manila Bay, Dewey's victory
    at, 61, 71
Manning, Lafe, 113
*Marblehead*, U.S.S., 76, 78, 81
Mare Island Marine Band, 19
*Marietta*, U.S.S., 58, 60, 62,
    63, 67
Markham, Henry Harrison,
    19
Martin, A., 26
Martinique, 67
*Masachusetts*, U.S.S., 13, 38,
    73, 76, 80, 83, 86, 97,
    100, 109
Massey Supply Corp., 121
*Mayflower*, U.S.S., 77
Melville, Engineer in Chief
    George W., quoted, 95–96
Menner, Capt. Robert T., 110

Merrell, Capt. John P., 105,
    106
*Merrimac*, C.S.S., (C.S.S.
    Virginia), 1, 8–9, 49
*Merrimac*, U.S.S., 76, 79, 84
Merritt, Maj. Gen. Wesley,
    100
Military forces, U.S.
    post-Civil War attitude
    toward, 3–4
Milligan, Chief Engineer
    Robert W., 31, 33, 56, 57,
    96, 126
*Minneapolis*, U.S.S., 73
*Mohican*, U.S.S., 52
*Monadnock*, U.S.S., 9, 45
*Monarch*, 18
*Monitor*, U..S., 1, 8–9, 49
Monitor ships, 8–9
*Monocaci*, U.S.S., 52
*Monterey*, U.S.S., 31, 34, 45,
    53
*Montgomery*, U.S.S., 74
Morris, E. T., 26
Morse, Wayne, 120
Murphy, J. A., 126
Murray, John, 26
*My Fifty Years in the Navy*
    (Clark), quoted, 56–57

Naval Construction Corp., 79
Naval Examination and
    Retirement Board, 99
Navy, British, in the 1880s,
    2–3
Navy, U.S.
    Civil War, 1–2
    post-Civil War, 2–4
*Newark*, U.S.S., 11
*New Hampshire*, U.S.S., 52
*New York*, U.S.S., 74, 75, 77,
    78, 80, 83, 86, 87, 89, 94, 100
New York *Journal*, 43, 47
New York *World*, 43, 47
*Niagara*, U.S.S., 26, 74
Nicholson, Lt. R. F., 90, 126

*Nictheory*, 60, 62, 64
North Atlantic Squadron, 73, 74
Northern Patrol Squadron, 73

Obry, Ludwig, 8
Offley, C. N., 126
Olcott, Ben Wilson, 109
*Olympia*, U.S.S., 26, 31, 61, 116
*Oquendo*, 88, 90
*Oregon*, U.S.S.
    armorplating of, 29–30
    arrival in New York Harbor, 100
    arrival in San Francisco, 105
    Barker becomes captain of, 98
    in the Battle of Santiago, 87–95
    becomes a memorial, 110–15
    in the blockade of Cuba, 77–80
    building of, 13, 15
    Clark becomes captain of, 48
    decommissioning of, 109
    description of, 123–26
    destruction of, 121
    distances covered in circumnavigating South America, 68–69
    on duty in the Philippines, 101–2
    on duty off the coast of China, 103–6
    launching of, 15–27
    sails from the West Coast to Key West, Fla., 55–68
    testing of, 31–38
    in World War I, 108
    in World War II, viii–ix, 115–19
*Ossippee*, U.S.S., 49–50
Overstreet, L. M., 126

Panama Canal, opening of, 107
Panama-Pacific Exposition (1915), 107
*Panther*, U.S.S., 81
Pengelly, R., 26
Pennock, Rear Adm. Alexander Mosley, 52
Pennoyer, Sylvester, 19
Perry, Commodore Matthew, 26
*Petrel*, U.S.S., 11
Philippines, insurrection in the, 100–102
Pierce, Walter M., 110
*Pluton*, 88
Pond, Capt. Charles F., 107
*Porter*, U.S.S., 74, 75
Portland, Ore., 110
Port Merizo, Guam, vii, 118–19
*Pride of the River*, 19
Public Law 523, 121
Pulitzer, Joseph, 43
*Puritan*, U.S.S., 9

*Ranger*, U.S.S., 52
Rankin, Capt. O. P., 110
Reeves, Comdr. Joseph M., 107, 126
*Reina Mercedes*, 97
*Rescue*, 19
*Resolute*, U.S.S., 95
Revolving gun turret, 1–2
*Richmond*, U.S.S., 50
Ricker, Edwin M., 117
Roberts, M. F., 126
*Rockaway*, 18
Rodman, Adm. Hugh, 108
Roosevelt, Franklin D., 109
    quoted, 116
Roosevelt, Theodore, 47, 69–70, 80, 106
Rough Riders (First U.S. Voluntary Cavalry), 80, 83, 85

Ruger, Gen. Thomas Howard, 18
Russian Revolution (1917), 108
Russo-Japanese War, 102, 105

Sadler, E. J., 76
*St. Louis*, U.S.S., 98
*St. Paul*, U.S.S., 77
Samoa crisis (1889), 12
Sampson, Adm. William T., 9, 58, 63, 66, 68, 73, 74, 75, 77, 78, 79, 83, 84, 98
Sandy Point, 59, 60
*San Francisco*, U.S.S., 73
San Juan, Puerto Rico, bombardment of, 74
San Juan Hill (Kettle Hill), battle of, 85
Santa Barbara Channel, 31
Santiago de Cuba, 77
  battle of (1898), 49, 87–96
Schackford, C., 76
Schley, Commodore Winfield S., 73, 76, 77, 78, 86, 89, 95
*Scindia*, U.S.S., 101
*Scorpion*, U.S.S., 76
Scott, Henry, 13, 21, 23
Scott, Irving M., 13, 20, 22, 23, 35 36, 38
  quoted, 21
"Seagoing coastal battleships," 12–13
*Sea King*, 19
*Sea Queen*, 19
Service Squadron 12, 118
*Sewanee*, U.S.S., 51
Shafter, Gen. William R., 82, 83, 97
Shanghai, China, 105–6
Shelby, Eugenia, 16, 17, 20, 22, 23
Sigsbee, Capt. Charles D., 46, 47
Simpson, Samuel L., 22

Slocum, Capt. Joshua, quoted, 65–66
Smith, A., 26
Snyder, Comdr. C. P., 108
Spain, start of war with, 60–62
Spanish fleet, destruction of, 87–96
Spar torpedoes, 7
Sprague, Charles A., 115
*Spray*, 65
Stone, Lt. C. M., 76
Sture, Richard, 26
Summers, Lionel M., 122

Telfer, W., 26
*Temerario*, 57, 59, 61
*Tennessee*, U.S.S., 50
Tenth Regular Cavalry, 83
*Terror*, U.S.S., 9, 74
*Texas*, U.S.S., 11, 73, 76, 86, 89, 95, 97
Thomas, Capt. Charles W., 105
Thompson, Mrs. Cora A., 113
*Tornado*, 42
Torpedo boat destroyers, 6–7
Torpedoes, 6–8
Tortugas, 72, 73
Tracy, Benjamin F., 11–12

*Ukiah*, 18
*Unadilla*, 34
Union Iron Works (San Francisco), 13, 15, 17, 32, 33, 35, 37, 105
United Spanish War Veterans, 113, 114
*United States*, U.S.S., 49
U.S. Marines, 81–82
U.S. War Production Board, 115

*Vanderbilt*, U.S.S., 51
Vaughn, William P., 24
*Vesuvius*, U.S.S., 76
*Vigilant*, 19

Villaamil, Adm. Fernando, 88
*Virginia*, C.S.S. *See*
   *Merrimac*, C.S.S.
*Virginius* affair, 42–43
*Vixen*, U.S.S., 76, 86, 94
*Vizcaya*, 46, 88, 90–92, 94

Waddell, Howard, 113
Wainright, Comdr. Richard,
   88
*Walla Walla*, 18
*Wampanoag*, U.S.S., 2
War of 1812, U.S. navy in
   the, 71
Washington Conference on
   Limitation of
   Armaments, 109
Watson, Commodore John
   Crittenden, 77, 98
Webster, Daniel, 42
Wettengil, Capt. I. C., 109

Weyler, Gen Valeriano, 43
Wheeler, Gen. Joseph, 83
Whitehead, Robert, 7
"White Squadron," 10
Wilde, Capt. George F. F.,
   103
Wilkes, Lt. Charles, 13
Williams, A. S., 126
Williams, Comdr. G. W., 107
*Wilmington*, U.S.S., 68
Wilson, Woodrow, 107, 108
*Wompatuck*, U.S.S., 74
Wood, Col. Leonard, 80
Worrell, Col. U. G., 113

*Yankee*, U.S.S., 81
*Yantic*, U.S.S., 52
Yarnell, H. E., 126
Yokosuka Naval Base
   (Japan), 121
*Yorktown*, U.S.S., 11